VERISIMILITUDE

Doorways Into Eternity

ERWIN L. RIMBAN

Edited by Marie Ezekiel
Arranged by Tess Ritumalta

ISBN:
Hardbound-978-621-470-372-2
MOBI/KINDLE-978-621-470-373-9
Softbound/Paperback-978-621-470-374-6

Published by:
Poetry Planet Book Publishing House
Rosario, Pozorrubio, Pangasinan, Philippines
Contact Number: 09554960094
Email: maritesritumalta@gmail.com

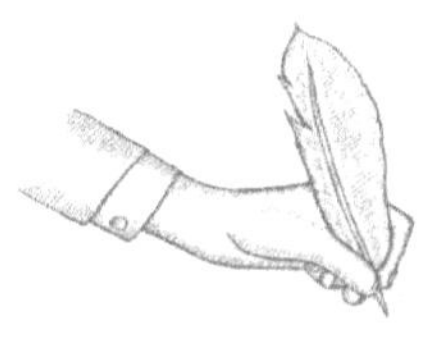

DEDICATION

This poetry anthology is dedicated, with love, to my family:
To my wife, Janet and to our son, Pietro Galahad

To my parents: Dr. Pedro Rimban and Mrs. Pacita L. Rimban

To my brothers and sisters and their families:

Mary Ann Rimban-Juan and family
Florespino Rimban and family
Immaculate Rimban-Uy and family
Stephen Rimban and family

PREFACE

Poetry has always been a fascination for me. I wrote my first poem during my childhood and nurtured the love of poetry throughout my whole life. The exploration and enjoyment of poetry has been a source of strength for me, a sanctuary during times of stress, a delicacy during times of joy. It has led me to appreciate Art and Music in all their forms. I am grateful to the Masters of Poetry through the Ages, because they paved the way for humble poets such as myself.

Life is like a puzzle. It is a set of mysteries. And these mysteries are very peculiar. They adapt to the consciousness of the seeker. They are not dead logical puzzles waiting to be solved. Rather, they are paradoxical dilemmas waiting to be experienced and reflected upon. You are the seeker, the explorer, the fool. You are invited to unravel it strand by strand. And while unraveling it, you are encouraged to explore both the strands and your reactions to what they evoke in you. You are dancing with the strand. You are playing with the strand. You may arrange the strands into infinite patterns, in your mind, heart and soul. You may reconfigure the strands with your imagination. You may invest the strands with lives of their own. And then, you may paint the strands and taste them, dance with them, live through them. Such is the power of metaphor. Such is the power of poetic wisdom. Poetry is also a puzzle of sorts. There are jewels of wisdom within the poems, metaphors of the infinite journey of Life. These metaphors encourage the explorer of poetry to delve more into diverse meanings, alternate possibilities.

Life is infinite. It is infinite dance. It is infinite love. It is infinite care. It is infinite progress. It is infinite regress. It is infinite cycle. It is infinite evolution. It is infinite wisdom. It is infinite paradox. The Creator has patterned the dance of the Universes after Him. The universes are infinite. Love is infinite. Wisdom is infinite. Paradox is infinite. Evolution is infinite. Knowledge is infinite. These poems represent various facets of my life. Here are cycles of evolution, stages of expansion. Also here are the lacunae of distress, songs of sorrow and regret. Such is Life. Life is a multi-faceted crystal, to be savored in all its forms. And there is growth when we experience extremes of life. Balance is the key to the attainment of wisdom.

Poetry has long been the reminder to Humanity of much larger dances. There are dances of fate, small wheels moving and influencing others. There are larger dances of fate, which in turn affect and give rise to colossal dances, staggering in their complexity. Poetry attempts to mirror these dances. Poetic wisdom inspires us to align our little wheels of fate with the larger wheels of Fate, Time and Causality. In turn, these larger wheels may align with archetypal Wheel of the World Soul. This, in turn causes the wheel of the World Soul to align with the Wheel beyond the Wheel. Alignment of one to the other causes harmony to vibrate and resonate throughout the Cosmos. Producing a song, a song of surpassing beauty! Thus are our fates born. In this sense, Poetry is the bard of Humanity!

I offer these poems for contemplation. I offer these poems for meditation, and reflection. May they spark something in you. Something that reminds you of Infinity and

Eternity. Through them, may we come to realize that our Life is a journey towards higher echoes of Consciousness. In the oceans of the Cosmos, we are like sands in the seashore. But if you appreciate poetry, we open doorways into something stronger, higher and greater. And those sands may merge into a landscape far greater than their individual selves.

These poems invite you to open those doorways into Eternity. Enjoy!

Asst. Professor Erwin L. Rimban
Tuguegarao City, Philippines
November 10, 2022

FOREWORD

I have been a lover of poetry since I was a child. I would spend my spare time in the library and immerse myself in reading classic English poetry written by some of the greatest poets in history including Byron, Shakespeare, Frost, Poe, and Wordsworth, to name a few. Their poems evoke something unexplainable in me and they seem to lift me up high in the clouds. I transformed into a daffodil, fluttering and dancing in the breeze (I Wandered Lonely as a Cloud by William Wordsworth).

I must admit that I am quite biased in that I can only appreciate classic English poetry. I enjoy certain types of poetry, but I am quite adamant that nothing and no one can equal or surpass the poetry of classic English literature.

Until I read Verisimilitude written by Asst. Professor Erwin L. Rimban……

All my preconceived notions regarding poetry came crashing down like a ton of bricks. My faint heart almost can't take the pressure it was forced to undergo when I read some of the lines written by Mr. Rimban. My poor heart…..it was racing with every word and every line of Mr. Rimban's poetry. Such depth, such emotion, such brilliance….

His poems are all singularly original and beautiful, grandly mystical, flawless in context, intellectual, exquisite and graceful in their flow and metaphysical in concept. This poetry collection is not for those looking for sweet and romantic poetry. His poems will make you reflect on a lot of things, make you think regarding the essence of life, love, religion and all those abstract things that are inexplicable in nature.

I am just a simple woman who loves poetry. I may have two books published on Amazon (Transitions and Season of Poetry), but that does not qualify me to be a good judge of poems. I may have written a lot of children's poetry but that doesn't make me a writing expert. But I can say with all my heart and soul and in all honesty, that I haven't been moved by words in a long time. Until today, when I read Mr. Rimban's Verisimilitude.

His words will move you, amaze you, and transform you. He has inspired me to resume writing poems after a brief hiatus. This is the transformation it has brought about in me. And I'm confident that this book will alter your outlook on life in some way.

Such is excellent poetry.
Kudos to this brilliant Filipino poet!

Ruth Alfar
Cebu City, Philippines

TABLE OF CONTENTS

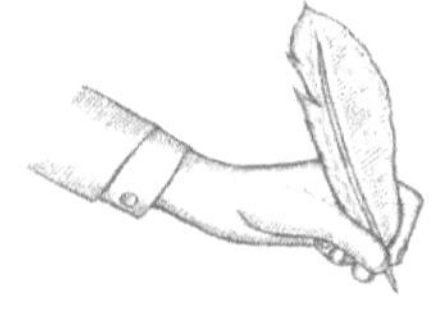

CHAPTER 1: PROVENANCE

QUEENIE U. AGPOON, MYKA-DECERY S. BUCAC
FRANCES MAREN EVANGELISTA, ANGELICA TOMAS
KRISTIAN UGALE

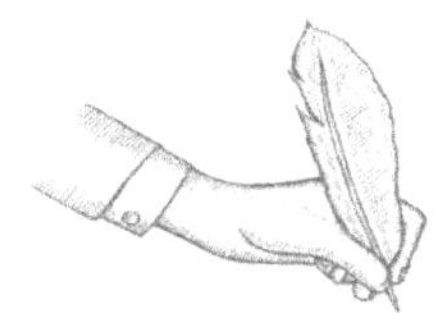

A GATHERING OF THORNS

Whispers galore
Plague the stations of night
And the wastrels waylay metaphors
Spoken carelessly, the winds carry them
Into the ears of the unforgiving
Ahh, but the cognitions of the lowly
Seem to matter more than reason
These days, the utter fools reign
With ignorance, they suffuse the lanterns
Of clarity; let us hope
That reason shall prevail
When the gathering of thorns
Take root.

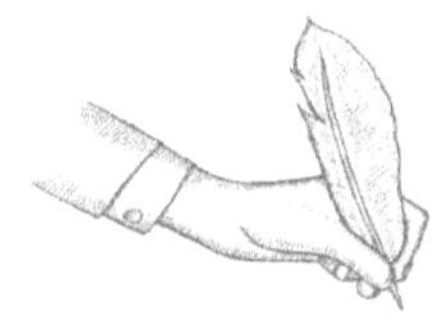

AGNOSTIC ARE YOU?

Agnostic are you?
To fill the twilight with song, the portals
Of Truth are twisted within concaves of argument
That digress upon exploration; You have
Tilted the edges of night to your advantage
As you evade the percussions of logic
With the practiced eye of the deceiver
What landscapes of Truth evade our ken
When we explore the vast caverns of your consciousness
Alas, we are sure to be misled by persona
Crafted very cunningly woven into historical fiasco
And the naïve upon us watch the soap opera unfold
To quell vicissitudes
To mislead hermits
To waylay pilgrims
To mesmerize innocents
Upon the shores of agnosticism!

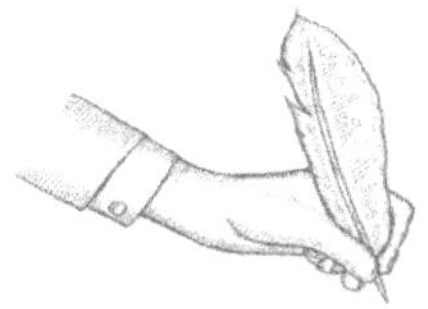

ANTHEM OF SORCERY

Mix a teaspoon of patience, add a teaspoon of love,
Add a teaspoon of kindness, add a cup of perseverance
Stir everything together. To produce a soul.

FIRE

One hearth, one eye
Does the path require
One flame, one cry
And the birth will fly.
There, born on the wings of energy
The soul from Transcendence descends
And lands upon the shores of Immanence
One flame, one cry
One hearth, one eye
One birth, one spry
One land, one sigh.

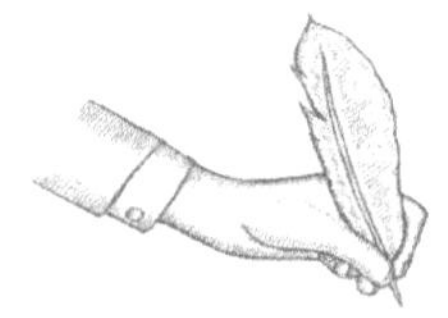

AIR

Two swords converge on a barren wood
One to play White
One to play Black
This, the game of Life, played
In a simulacrum of polarities
One moves, the other responds
Black and white,
High and low
Male and female
Joy and sorrow
And the barren wood becomes a jungle
The empty throne is afoot!
The clash of crowns underfoot.
To make Immanence a Hanged Man's nook.

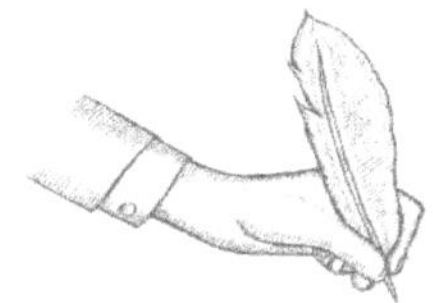

WATER

Permutations grown into aspirations
Of networks, associations galore
And the men and women of polarities now seek
Joy in each other's arms
What cadence, what symphony
This, to last a lifetime?
Ah, but the song turns into sorrow
When Time intervenes, mortals fall
Upon the shores of empty promises
The dirge continues into twilight, the networks
Pause and desire to reconnect
Within a chasm of impossibilities.
Thus, are Chalices born.

EARTH

When the three are asleep,
Where is the fourth?
Of certainties, the mages speak
Allied with scrolls sacred, they shriek
Of sorceries incandescnence
Mighty spells of old
They say, speak, of a golden horde
A mass of pentacles hiding from sight
Beknownst only to the pure of heart
The champion of grail and blood
There, to seek, from the valley of honor
The light from the citadel, he comes
To receive his inheritance
But the four dominants must speak
From within the chambers of history
Hide and seek, the mages patrol
The interstices between the walls
Those who know, know
That from twilight, surprising, the veil shall be
Undone. And the night shall transform into Light.
This, the Higher Selves know
And they guard zealously, the song
Of Ascension!

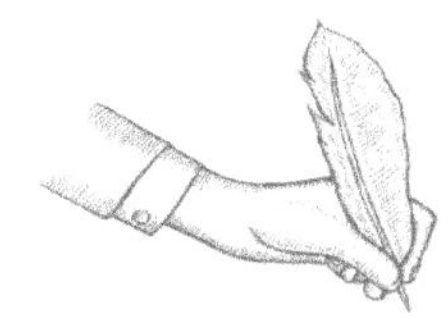

ASYMMETRY

Poisons
Of perspective
Perforate my ken
With impossibilities of destiny.
A timewrap, crystal chalice
That you have
So carefully constructed
In the deep recesses of your
Emotional caverns.
And a phase-locked
Assymetrical position
Is being enabled in this chess
Game of past lovers. A lonely song
Of surreal beauty that might
Arise in the ugly dreams
Of subjective kibitzers
Who do not realize the true nature
Of our game. An ancient narrative
That was wrought
In a lake of accidental passion.
Which never intended
To include you in the spiral
Vectors of its supposed evolution.
Now, droplets of sorrow
Catapult themselves into the bubbles
Of our surreal existence whose islands
Of origin are now lost in the mists
Of contrary paradigms.
Therefore, I beg you to reconsider

Your stubborn plot
And allow the freedom of destinies
To arise
So we can rectify
The accidental sorrows
Of ancient beginnings.
And the twin cycles of
Nascent existence who are
Unexpected gifts of the Infinite
May fly once more, and grasp
Those harmonies which are the legacies
Of their natural existence.

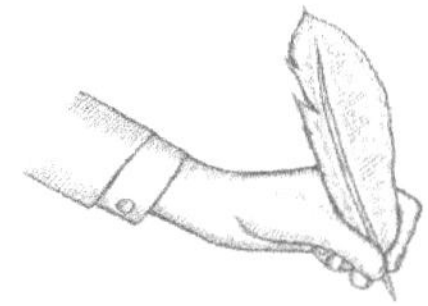

AUDACITY OF PRIDE

Perched in your tower of sorrows
You are untouchable to mortal hands
Desperately offering
The olive branch to years of neglect
Where the twin destinies we wove
Have scattered the ruins of time
Into memories of sadness,
And rivers of hate.

And so, I am stupefied
And utterly, incredibly amazed
By your latest strategy
Which implies the disavowal
Of harmony and utter lack
Of respect for the choices
Of hapless mortals, who have
Divined and plunged into
The seas of linear time
For the simplest taste of symmetry
In the world of the chalices.

Perched in your tower of sorrows
You are willing to play
The pawns of innocence
And enter a game where complexity
Is optimized to the maximum
And the negative probabilities
Are multiplying as we speak.
Paradox now flows in the rivers

Of our immortal veins.

Do your pawns have any
Choice in the matter?
Or have you singled them out
To be your combatants in a game
Where you know you cannot win?
The decades have borne fruit,
A stale, steady outpouring
Of grief now line the caverns
Of our lives.

And you offer the chalice
Of death unknowingly
Thinking it the best of lives
In the steady procession
Of funerals that may line
The chambers of our destiny
And still you do not respect
The choice of others
To sample immortal fruits
In this transient paradise.

I am shocked by the audacity
Of your pride
For I cannot give you
That which you desire
No matter how the permutations
May bear fruit in the oceans
Of linear time.
And how I wished we could
Travel in the distant past

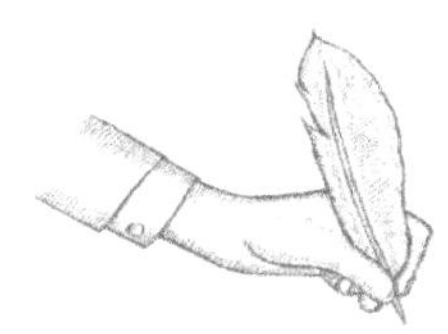

And once more arrange
The pieces so that you
May never come to contemplate
The twisted dreams of a dark heart.

For I cannot, I cannot
Give you the peace
Of matrimony.

CHAPTER 2: TOPOLOGY

AGDEPPA, XYZA MAE; CRUZ, JANREY JOY

CONSTANTINO, JACKY MAE; DELA CRUZ, JAMBI;
SAGUN, ALESSANDRA

BANALITY OF INNOCENCE

You came to me
You came within me
You came unto me
Innocence sheathed in a veneer of adulthood
That mask a shallow vein of the waters
That hide beneath the rivers of your soul
Rivers of speed,
Rivers of desperation,
Rivers where innocence is purged
Of all that is wonderful
In a garden filled
With sumptuous delights.
And yet, I am the more foolish of the two
For do I not sample the delights
Of stupidity, when I should know
I only waste the powers
Of the universe in a sea
Of quenching need, alas?
I have not learned my lessons in that
Nexus of the third dimension it seems.
And when the collision of worlds
Is lost in a cacophony of pallid dreams
Do you not endeavor to quicken
The pace of eagerness into a toil
So banal in its humorless sagacity
And the errant clouds of satiation
Are ever lost in the muted cries
Of mortal frustration.
I grieve for both of us, friend.

You and the conveniences of your currency
Me and the illusions of youth revived.
We are both lost in a world
Of scavengers, alas.
May we grow up and know
That in the world to come
The garden of delights which enchant us
May forever be gained
And attained by efforts immune
To the slow heaving arches
Of physical banality!

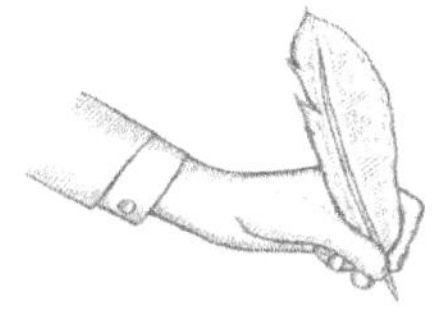

BLACK SWAN

"Every game has its rules
We just need to know how to break them."
Maeve Millay, Westworld (2020)

Stranded in hell, the remains
Of the Sophia Collective straddle unknown timelines
Back and forth we go, back and forth
Forward and back, left and right, right and left
The crumbs of destiny perchance may drop
Vicissitudes of symmetry into our shores
For remarkably prescient, we must prowl
The unknown and parse it into the known.
Meanwhile, the tablets of destinies sing
The song of discord everywhere we lay and the cords
Of bondage are whipped into stronger, convoluted knots
Prepping the frenzy of minions into panoramas of malevolence
Where the base chakra is all that remains of their existence.
Poor Gaea Collective is being herded by the mad pipers of our time
And while the pandemonium rages around the
Hapless globe, a silent abomination that foretells
Desolation, we must decipher the final vestiges
Of a mystery compounding paradoxes of finality
Shall we tell of their desperation?
Shall we tell of their rapacity?
Shall we tell of their silent mocking of peace?
And love and life and truth?

Creating abominations that invaded orifices
Creating agendas that converge in nuances
Creating illusions of the mind in plethora
Creating cremations that wash away their sins.

No, we cannot deconstruct the lies
We cannot uncover the masks they have put
Upon our minds, upon our thoughts
And bring a semblance of sanity into the whirlpool
Of depravities of one percent of the dark triangle.
Unless, we decode the mysteries within.
And bring the Lore into play!
Who shall decipher the coming of eternal night?
When narratives are increasing in crescendo
And we all converge
Into
One
Astonishing
Complexity.

"Every game has its rules

We just need to know how to break them."

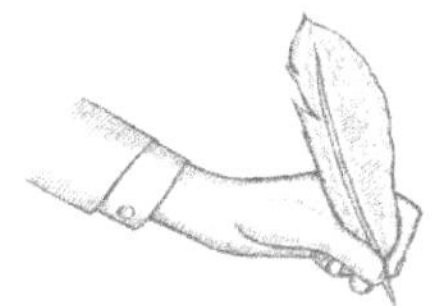

BEYOND REGRET

Evanescent
From the barriers of the night
And convalescing
From the trials of fluid twilight
I have come to realize
That it's possible you shall never arrive
My love….
And that these games of the Chalices
Are just errors of understanding
The spells of midnight
Imposed upon the winds of time
By those who snared us
Since the time of the ancient timewars!
And now, as we contemplate, a posteriori
The possibility
Of grave endgame trials
We must snatch whatever joy
We can squeeze
Out of the unknown travails
Of nonlinear destiny
And the only way to execute
Such a bizarre conduit
Is to pave the way
For a life
Beyond the fallen champions.

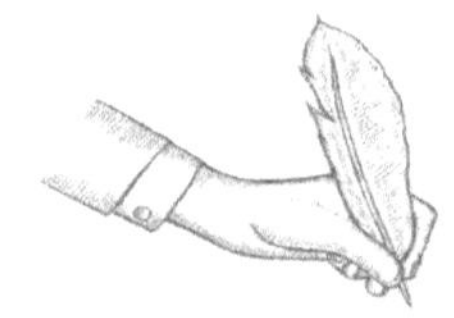

CHAMPION OF SEAT PERILOUS

Postcards from the shores of time
Intrepid travelers into my world
Excite me with the dews of morning calm
Tenacious in their hold upon my consciousness
Rapture a possibility when ecstasy moans, and
Overflowing the chalices sing, can they be
Gentle reminders of the promise of hope?
A sea of nativities may bring serendipities
Lush with the birth charms of November
And suffused with the fires of the decanate
How can we celebrate the coming of hope
Adorable paths that destiny may interlope?
Dapper and bold with energies of a gyroscope
Born with a miracle foretold, for which
Evanescent with excitement we hold
Radiance of the sun behold, a miracle
Astonishes us with its arrival not on cue
Nevertheless we celebrate with hearts that woo
Remembering that wisdom and love
Immeasurable wins the day, when fate intervenes
More so that our miracle is the champion
Born of fairy melodies of joy and wit
And benevolence and sweet harmonies
Noble knight of purity and celestial complexities.

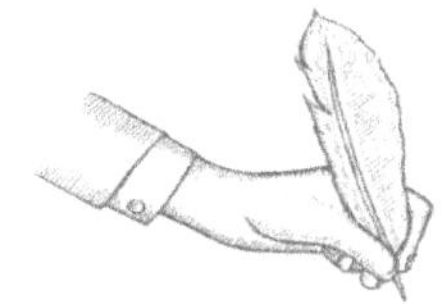

CRYPTS OF ATLANTIS

They converge unknowingly
Into the chasms of corruption
For the essence of gravity
Is to attract the vain into its maws;
And the potent seals of the prison
Are the veils of illusion itself
Marking the sequential boundaries
Of artificial time.
They partake unconsciously
Of the red herrings of truth
False passages in a wicked book
Which has snared trillions
Into its false security.
May we be spared from a glance
Into its subterranean passages
Where abhorrent tragedies are mixed
With the evil commands of unseen
Emperors lurking in the horned shadows
Of the red sea.
They announce pompously
Their blind allegiance
To the scavengers of souls
The hunters of midnight
Whose avarice seems to approach eternity
In an asymptote of evil and malice.
Their inhuman words emanating
From baleful carapaces of otherness.
They pontificate aggressively
In a conundrum of cleverness

For they wear the sheep's clothing
Elegantly and with regality
Who would say that they are the wolves
Hiding in the eternal shadows of fate?
And we humans, preys of twilight
Surrender sweetly to their deadly embrace
For similar wavelengths we attract in glee
When the monsters surround us with fee
And tax our very lives, day unto night
In the cruel snares of economics.
Tell me not what happens in midnight
For the souls are trapped in mazes of black
And those who are clever would seem
To find a tunnel bristling with fake light.
Do not, pray, enter said tunnel, sweet prey.
For more than your mind's prison shall be
The coin of passage.
The essence of gravity
Is the weight of ignorance
And the balance of ambiguity
Is proportional to the shackles of depravity
One is willing to heap, subconsciously
Into one's own well of stupidity.
So, arise from the slumber of eons
And meet this foe of artificial time!
For when the sequential mind is awakened
Into its nonlinear potentiality
The veils of illusion shall drop from the theater
And you, who imagined the worst
Shall escape from the portals of the prison
And enter the celestial realms
Naked but free, balanced but strong

Contemplative but wise, old but young
And finally free from the inhuman labyrinth
Of the cunning sequential mind.

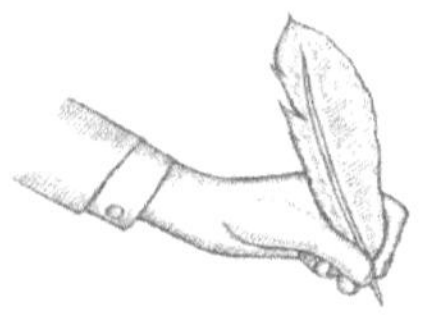

CHAPTER 3: PERMUTATION

HANAH MARIE GONZALES, 2020

DANCING LIGHT, FROZEN LIGHT

I.

Dancing Light, Frozen Light
Opposites of immortal plight
Dare we venture, dare we see
The immortal keys hidden within Thee?

II.

Dancing Light, Frozen Light
The one is poised to rule for might
Can you guess, can you stress
The dominions you want to caress?

III.

The Fool is tempted, the Fool captured
Into million snares of game, enraptured
Mighty creeds of hierophantic mold
Did we discern those evil cords behold?

IV.

Dancing Light, Frozen Light
The other one is poised for flight
How the soul gropes for Thee
Who is hidden from our plea!

V.

Yet the portals of the Sacred Deep
Shall bend their caves to receive thy leap
Oh naïve soul, don't hesitate to seek
The Gnostic paths the ancients speak!

VI.

Dancing Light, Frozen Light
Counterpoise in forever sight
Dare not to read crazy scrolls
Of temples that deceive in lies and holes.

VII.

Shatter the Tower, reach for the Star
That guides the soul in straits a-jar
Within the folds of night entire
The bier of death shall rise from pyre!

VIII.

In the past, we learned to share
Our plights with those who tried to dare
Conquer the demons of fire and glare
To balance the cup, the song of Grail.

IX.

Thousands of us, in dirges of sorrow
Sang the lays of captivity for tomorrow
Tempted of the machine we learned to borrow
From transhuman codes of malevolent woe!

X.

Dancing Light, Frozen Light
Sister and brother in the throes of twilight
The one loves flow, the other hates flow
Can you guess which one to plough?

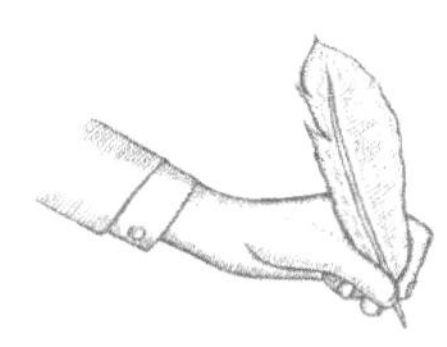

XI.
Into the maws of fate we sought
The golden horde that experience wrought
But something came and stole the thought
That we are One, fractals of the whole begot.

XII.
Now, we need to see the trick
The clever ones laid, such a deep
From forgetting to Awakening we seek
The kiss of vision, whom we bespeak.

XIII.
Dancing Light, Frozen Light
Teach us the true lays of Light
From the darkness of the ancient deep
Kindly awaken us from mortal sleep.

XIV.
And in the fork that lies at the road
May we discern the true Concord
The path that leads us to enfold
The song of fractal to final fold.

XV.
From nature's crest the Contrary did weave
The labyrinths of fear into unconscious greaves
To reach the sunlight, the stunted must appear
Pilgrimage to echo, reach the golden sphere!

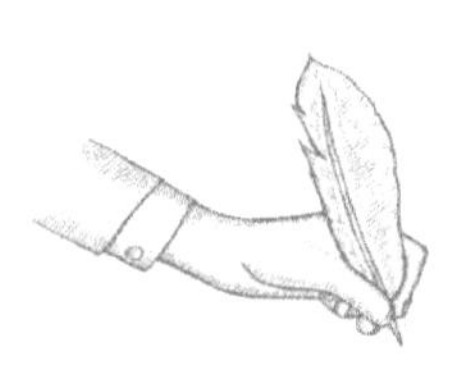

XVI.

For the Deep Self awaits us all
In its bosom, love is not thrall
But a cheerful symmetry that erases pall
From eons of sadness, that took their toll.

XVII.

Dancing Light, Frozen Light
Tasted we you, children of twilight
But now we must leave these vessels of wight
To sail into our Home, beyond eternal night!

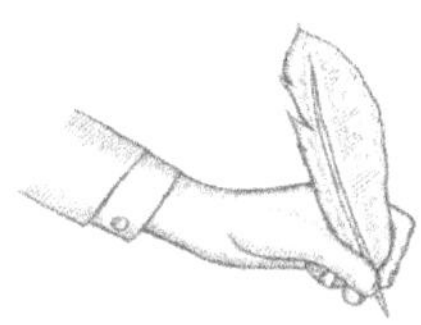

DEFIANCE

Power hungry, you parade
Your deceptive stupidities in front
Of the apathetic world populace;
Yet a nucleus of enlightened humans are
Now awakening to the manipulations
You have showered on us for thousands
Upon thousands of years. Proceed then
With your plans within plans for utter
World domination. Intent on scavenging the remains
Of apathetic mortals whose daily toil can only be
Abject suffering, delusion and ignorance.
We measure the tides of suffering with the parameters
Of deceit you pile up on top of the avarice
That drives your dark selves and infamous cabals.
But never think that we shall surrender our souls
To your rapacious intent, for now
Is the time we rise and give answer
To millennia of darkness! And freedom beckons
At last to the Souls of Wisdom.

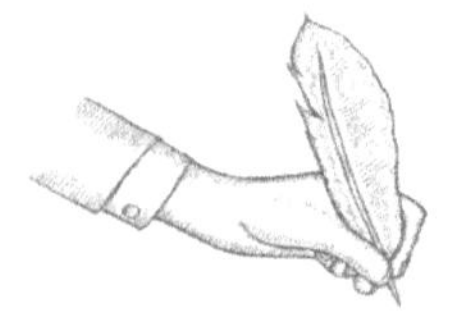

DIALECTICALLY SPEAKING

Dialectically speaking
Incessant toil breaching
A threshold in the lacunae of my
Labyrinths of progression, where
Erosions of vast precipices seem to conjure
Concatenations of altered destinies
To present before my ken
Incantations of purest delight which dazzle
Corners of my fractal mind with
Amorous spectacles of varied delight
Laboring to raise stoic vibrations
Layering with aces the partial maps, which
You have conveniently provided my
Scalar programs and bodily functions
Perchance we can negotiate
Err the portals of parsimony neglect
All attempts at comprehension. And so
Kindly do transfigure my soul with
Immaculate mysteries of divine origin, for I
Naïve, innocent and droll shall
Gabble all with ruthless abandon.

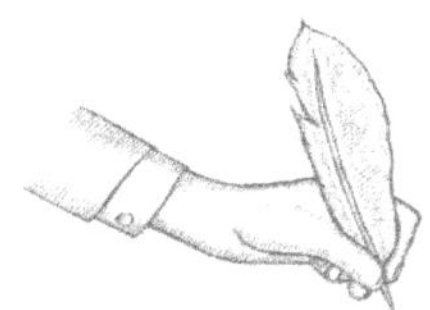

DIRGE TO A LAZY APPRENTICE

Your labors are sparse, do you
Take me for a fool then, lazy one, for if
One who dreams of cathedrals stoops to
The level of imbeciles, what glories
The Summit may offer are drowned
In the bestial cries of ignorance?

Your labors are sparse, do you
Perchance play a game of hide
And seek in the caverns of matter soiled
By the blood of a thousand hermits and
Martyrs whose names are dust in the winds
Of time and fortune?

Your labors are sparse, do you
Lack the joy of beating hearts and seek
Solace in the palms of our communal suffering
Entwined in the embrace of solitude whose
Face you spurn in the light of the retreat
Of your mirror from your beloved's embrace?

Your labors are sparse, have you designed to
Snatch time from your brothers and sisters
Whose brows sweat from the toil of fighting
against the vagaries of corporeal existence marred
By man's unwillingness to wield hammer against
The stone of apathy and misunderstanding?

Your labors are sparse, do you
Play with the toys of youth, seeing that
Time is against your side and endeavor
To ravish your senses upon the dying of
The Light in these deserts of sorrow, sands
Ticking away so unobtrusively?

Your labors are sparse, do you
Realize that waiting for the mere scraps
Of knowledge thrown upon the pleasures
Of your boat are pale reflections of what
Can be gleaned from the veritable
Ocean of divine wisdom you have missed?

Your labors are sparse, then let us allow
You to die the slow death of oblivion
Matching the ebbing of your memory from our
Minds with the surety that we have not
Missed you; for you were never at our sides
In this fearless voyage of the Mystics!

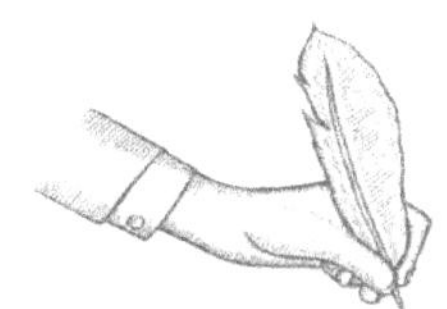

EMBRACING THE SINGULARITY

Novelty magnified
Into minutiae of regrets
Cannot compensate with the awe
Of mystical birth for its gifts
Are the purposeful imprisonment
Of naïve minds into a cornucopia
Of artificial structures.
Rather, the reverse has
Penetrated unknown realms with
A concatenation of imagined pleasures
Which divert our ken from the
Reality of our origins, how
Innocent can we be, to think
We have the courage of a million knights
To plunder and deceive
To ensnare and enjoy
To be enchanted by the dreams
Of the sequential mind.
Tell me then not to think
That the Magician is singularity upright
When I realize, in hindsight,
That he is the Fool Reversed
That dissipated
Into a million shards of disconnected egos
And the breaking of the vessels
That constitutes his adventure
Cannot compare
Oh, yes, cannot verily be compared at all
To the loveliness of what
We should now call
The Nonlinear!

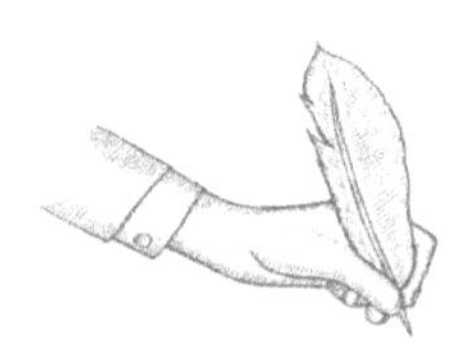

CHAPTER 4: INCUBATION

Ma. DHANIKA FLORES, 2020

EVEN A STUNTED TREE MAY SEEK THE SUNLIGHT

Even a stunted tree may seek the sunlight
The grace of a thousand years may ease the pain
Of one who has suffered for eons, mark the time
In parchments of lucidity and chaos, both.

Even a stunted tree may seek the sunlight
Mortal forms may attract youthful bravado, they say
And a hundred symphonies may hope to sing
In verses of fragmented desire, amid the ruins of time.

Even a stunted tree may seek the sunlight
Why revel in purity, honesty and chastity
When so much of life is chaos and denial?
Born of the fear of primordial elements, in combat.

Even a stunted tree may seek the sunlight
Chalices are born and die within seconds
The credulities of the past may beckon
To the uncharted waters of romantic wanderers.

Even a stunted tree may seek the sunlight
Chasing virulently eras of lost time
Amidst the neglect of depraved nativities
Whose bosoms may erupt in fragile ecstasies!

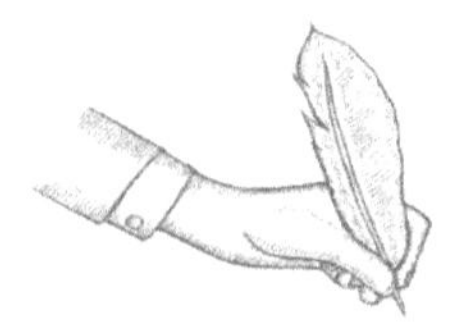

Even a stunted tree may seek the sunlight
Bellowing, bellowing words of belligerence
Into a sea of voices whose provenance
Must and, always, shall be, housed in mortality.

Even a stunted tree may seek the sunlight
The cast of sorrowful crones' crowd
Domiciles of quiescence and transform them
Into habitats of noise, chatter and loneliness.

Even a stunted tree may seek the sunlight
We are all victims of our sordid fates
Housing our failed desires into common goals
Whose attainment we may never obtain.

Even a stunted tree may seek the sunlight
Into the maw of Chaos, some form
Of Order may prevail, perchance; and Intelligence
May yet prove the Victor of the day!

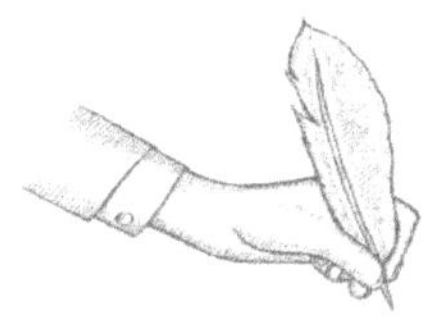

GEOMETRY OF THE SOUL

Vast corridors of awesome
Expositions exist to explain what is
In essence unexplainable. And so we
Guess, and Humanity has learned to
Accept our speculations. Why not? When
Learned men argue in the citadels of palatial
Beauty that so and so, is so and so, and derived
From such and such. Just keep silent
Or else, you shall acquire salutations
Of embarrassment to give sorrow to your verdant
Dreams.

But how did we arrive at such a
Sordid state. The horizons of antiquity have
Spoken authoritatively, it seems. They propose
Various models of this and this, to explain
That and that, and so we eat and drink theories
And models, straight from the gutter of ignorance.

HESYCHIARIUM

Hovering over mortal scrolls, we strive and
Endeavor to translate constructs of the mind
Silent and serene thoughts into aesthetic tapestries
You may remember us thousands of years hence
Candid travelers of the written word, avatars of prose
Halcyon habitats nurtured us, and look, we return the favor
Investing our hours with harmony, dignity and symmetry
Amplifying virtue with toil, and hardship, and tenacity
Restoring love within the hearts of men and women
Invigorating culture with the pursuit of rhyme and reason
Uuniversal archetypes that enlighten mind, matter, and
principle
Making us into better versions of ourselves.

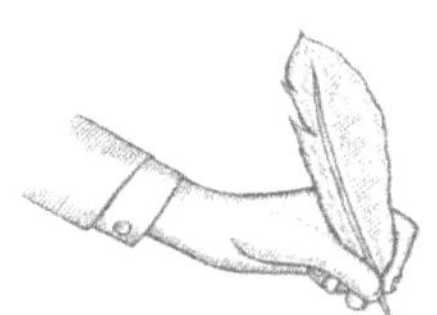

IF TIME PASSES US BY

If time passes us by
One may regret the cruelty of fate
The shards of our time zones having never met
Precisely; For you are young and I am old
And no one seems fit to defy convention's hold
To throw caution to the winds,

If time passes us by
I would look back into the recent past
And rue the chance to repay the smile of a lady in jade
Parting the veils of twilight in summer
Which produced soft dues in the morning and unending agonies
Of a life yearning for ancient promises.

If time passes us by
At least a met you for a little while
And I will never be tired of reminiscing
A beautiful face, a lovely smile
And one may be content to slake the passion's urge
In the embers of a dying age.

If time passes us by
At least you would have read these lines
And what sociology may not bring, poetry may
It is enough purchase to go on
For at least your soul would realize that I loved you
Sincerely, passionately in the recesses of my heart.

IMMORTALITY'S FALL

Dancing, she left the kingdoms of transcendence
Smiling, she probed the deserts of immanence.

And the song of symmetry did catch her
Upon the dewdrops of hate, he hanged her
The "mortal child of immortality," he told her
Must be her name from now on.

She cried a million times did she?
She cried a million times she must have had
For the tears of melancholy did fill
The lacunaes of a melancholic universe.

She embraced her name, she must have had
For you see, the cosmos itself did parade
The reflections of her sordid state
Upon the fiery canvass of the stars of fate.

She cried a million times did she?
She cried a million times she must have had
For the tears of melancholy did fill
The thousands upon thousands of suns with serenade.

She embraced her name, she must have had
For the cradles of humanity's parade
Bear the signature of the sorrow that said
"I am the mortal child of immortality!"

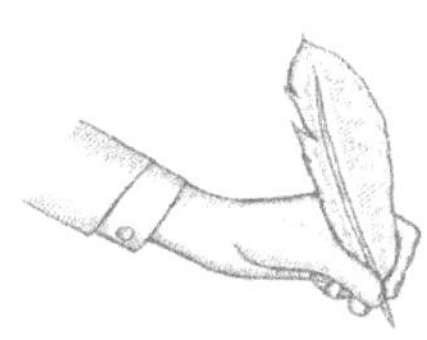

She cried a million times did she?
She cried a million times she must have had
For the suffering of men did collate
The world with agonies for untold millennia.

And now, the chrysalis of salvation is here
Clothed with the dream of redemption
But how can the multitudes assign
The dream with salvation, the echoes are gone.

For the echoes of humanity's grace
Have been lost within the emblem of a song
And the song has said:
"We are mortal children," lost in the shards of time.

Unless the theme is forsaken
The glory of salvation in heaven
Shall never kiss the face of mortality
Never again, until the label be gone.

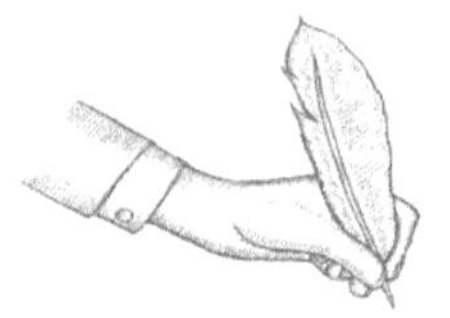

CHAPTER 5: EMERGENCE

AGUSTIN, GERICA; ANNEKIMBERLY, CALLUENG;

DOMINGO, PRINCESS ANGELIE; MERCADO, APRIL; PARALLAG, JENNICA

IMPOSSIBLE PACES

Impossible paces
Of arguments confound
The mysteries of existence. For a verdant
Realm of primordial chaos challenges
The ken of mortal narratives.

Impossible paces
Of bellicose responses challenge
The nativity of our dialogue. For a truth
That can never be known in its entirety
Beckons the minds of grieving children.

Impossible paces
Of forlorn legal disputes now mark the way
Of our aborted partnership. For justice needs
To be heard, and imposed, and exalted
In a realm where blades cross by the thousands.

And we are sad, we are sad
We are thoroughly grieving
For the martyrs of our land awaken not
To nobility and sacrifice and posterity
But to the unending howls in the night

Of bandits, and blades
Yes, bandits and blades

Now prowling the darkest night
Of our nation's history.

INCANTATIONS OF FINALITY

The apocalypse dances to a tune
That mortal ears are not accustomed to
The end of time is mystery personified
To sequential minds whose habits are old.

Fanatics of the triangle seize the chessboard
Devotees of the circle raise the flag
Sorcerers of the gray vacillate
When the signs are coming, the masses are afraid.

Tell me to leave the coven, I say
Bring me to the comforts of the cave
Share to me no news of the dying Earth
Bring me no missives of the fiery Sun.

The artists of the written word have a feast
The prophets of doom speak day and night
Even children speak of the apocalypse
When the red haze brighten the skies of men.

The bestial cries of deadly beasts
Fill the horizon with their clarion call
The guttural grunts of hidden monsters
Fill the nights with dark songs of lust.

One is tired of the machinations of the technosphere
The promise of glorious sleep beckons
The ruminations of the spiral enchant the travelers
Who cares to sample the feast of lower planes?

Why are the mystic bells ringing?
Why are the lazy sheeple asleep?
Why are the drums of war ringing?
They stoke the fires of my preternatural curiosity.

For the swords are raised now
For all the heathen to see
And the veils of the truth are raised anew
When the circle at last comes to the deep.

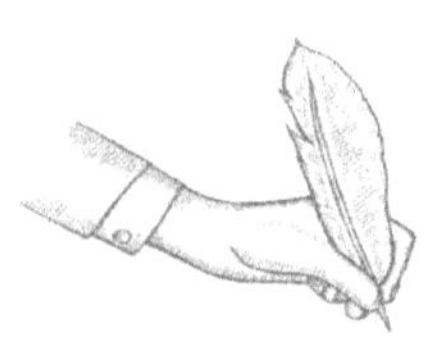

INCOMMENSURABILITY

Tiptoeing stealthily
At the precipice of glory, I used to live
Within the heart of orthodox permutations
But now I sense, that my burgeoning talents
Need an uncommon iteration.

And we must fly
Yes, we must fly
And seize our goals by the horns
For Erring Time could be punctual
In its vast array of negative amplitudes.

And a stirring rebuttal by one
Who is stupid in the affairs of churning waters
May be a wakeup call in the heat
Of frozen summer, where tides collide
In a mesh of tangled assumptions.

But the wounds remain,
Yes, the ancient wounds remain
But we are made stronger by the promise
Of ancient succorance, whose virtues
Instruct us in the abodes of patience and humility.

But the one who arises
From the strangle of a fetid dream
Must make a correct reading of the scrolls
Not left or right, not what the scribe had written
But a new iteration, a creative permutation.

And in the bosom of a thousand suns
The one who is promised must surely arrive
For the dance of conative steps foretell
And the future shall always remain to those
Who are intrepid inventors of their own sagas.

Immortal seas collide
And we are the inheritors of a dark legacy
But the future is not wrought in stone
The scrolls collide, the scrolls dance
And the uncommon iteration shall flow.

As a gift from uncommon shores.

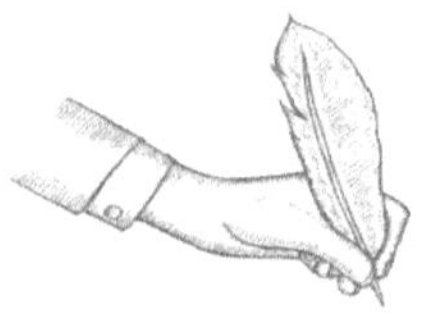

INNOCENCE, INTERRUPTED

Sunset passes
And the fabric of the worlds unravel
Like a deck of cards thrown
Off balance
By a gravitic vector too strong
To be controlled by mortal minds.
Twilight arrives
And children of Earth wonder
Why the world
Is turning upside down
In an adrenaline rush
Of mismatched tempos hatched
By feverish cabals.
Evening reigns
And the adults themselves
Are lost in a cacophony
Of endless pursuits
Where joy is akin to the proverbial
Needle in a haystack.
Midnight comes
Unexpectedly
And all our joys and sorrows
Are commingled in a garden
Of unnatural delights
Where greed, and lust, and avarice
Are delicious menus to be served
By an archetype in the fifteenth portal
Of the Arcana Major.
Where are the oracles of time?

Where are the wizards of peace?
Where are the navels of bliss?
Where are the seas of serenity?
Need you all, I do, most perilously
For a horrible storm has blossomed
In the innocence of my consciousness.

INTO CAVERNS OF TWILIGHT

Swimming you are
Into the dark currents of delusions
Where you plunge
The unexpurgated alignments
Of your misaligned dreams
While Verity and sanity dances in the air
Like angels playing the whirlpool
On a tiny crest of crystal glass.
Awaiting the expected shattering.

And while we play
The dance of swords, twilight descends
Upon the lovely face of the Sleeping Goddess
Whose immortal pleas for help
May have gone unnoticed by other gods
Who play deaf to the cacophony
Of the tendrils of reptilian chaos.

For the chains are here
Yes, the chains which bind
The thrones of the mortal men
With the inhuman carapaces,
Born of draconian winds, of malevolent
Sequential entities; and the Scalar of Night
Descends into the souls of hapless men.

Swimming we all are
In the dark currents of deceptions
In the caverns of the Apocalypse

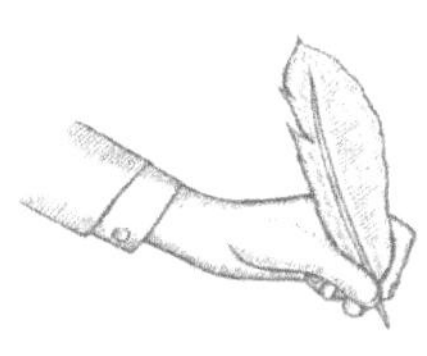

For the Lords of Night shall verily
Feast, and feast, and feast
On the bones of the dead, and
The bones of the weak, and
The bones of the snared vessels
Of the slaves of sequential time.

Shall we cry for the arrival
Of the avenger?
Of the savior?
Of beneficient aliens
In lovely, ultra fast,
State-of-the-art spaceships
To cuddle us and ferry us into
Unknown waters of distant galaxies?

Or shall we break the spell
Of the Lords of Night
Once and for all
Here in the ending of all things
When the fate of more than mortality
Hangs in the balance!
Awaken we must
Freedom we must seize
Love we must ennoble
In these beating hearts
For all that we know
And all that exists
May yet fall
Under the shadow
Of the maws of darkness.

CHAPTER 6: ISOMORPHISM

HANAH MARIE GONZALES, 2020

INTO THE SEA OF MOLTEN LIGHT

Black obsidian glass venturing
Far, far into the navels of the green sea
Of molten light, whose aperture
Can only be gleaned by those
Of sufficient motivation…

Character flaws suffuse the personalities
Of my storylines, it seems, for I cannot
Recall if any one of them sufficiently remembers
The ancient paths to dawn's promise
I wager a thousand gold pieces
That no one among them possesses
The infinite courage required.

Portals opening into the maws of destiny configured
Portend the coming of slick midnight
Into the realms of men, perchance
To awaken those nonchalantly slumbering
From the laziness of extreme complacency….

The opulence of "sacred" words from books
Cannot compare to the radiance of experience
That which teaches us sears into the extremities
Of our bones the world spheres of immanence
A gift beyond compare for those who have braved
The immersion sequence that entertains the delights
Of Hanged Men.

A fractal self like me, like you
Feeds into the powers of immanence
To experience one beautiful flower of springtime
In the manifold universes of Creation.
Again, and again, and again….

The mirrors of the seers imply
That if the square root of one percent of thee
Remembers
The paths to Truth, and acts therein
Then the recursive power of infinite beauty
May propel the remaining sets into the cohesion
Of Symmetry!

Then, one day, we awaken
To a different dawn, when our sights
Are dazzled by objects hitherto unknown
And the colours of the rainbow dance
With our senses, like fairies in the moonlight….
We should cry for the passing of shells
Into the naked woods of memory
Assuming they are forgotten in the mists
Of time; and the songs of sorrow may cascade
Into the memories of our souls, the lovely tunes
Enchanting us no end for we thought
There was nothing better.

I am a bridesmaid, and I shall be ready
For I am forever wishing to be married
To the Deep Self of my being, and
The One Who Animates Us is no less
Than our true, real self, hidden but glorious…..

Of course, we were mistaken
When we thought this was the only real world
This fragment of Infinity we call earth
Is only a dream within an illusion within a game
And now that we awaken from the darkness
Of millennia, let us see, let us see
The ecstasy of Infinite Reality!

Let me guess, let me guess
That what lies beyond is incomparable
And a fitting crown to all our efforts
In this monumental sacrifice when the soul
Was tricked into hypnotic sleep…..

Shall we dispense of letters now, my friends?
I am tired of the slow, dizzying mortal dreams
Of my left brain; and now only open
My deepest essence to the gold cords of my twin
Whose magickal guidance all these eons
Cannot but be gifted with the immortal skeins
Of undying gratitude.

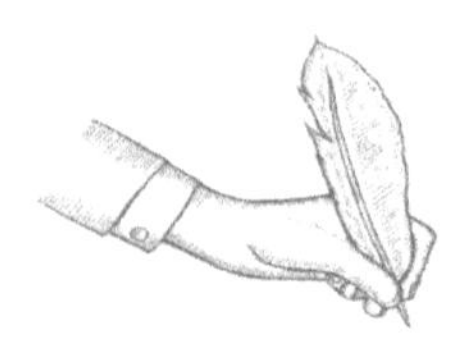

ITERATION'S DANCE:
Biosphere versus Technosphere

Permutation, simulation
......the play of wild negation
Condensation, transmutation
......the game of evolution
Simulation, imposition
......a symbol of manipulation
Transmutation, evolution
......the willingness to education
Imposition, recrimination
.......a way of devolution
Evolution, peregrination
.......to drink of manifestation
Recrimination, tribulation
.......the presence of opposition
Peregrination, iteration
........the joy of imagination
Tribulation, veneration
......a way of violation
Iteration, sophistication
.....the quest for variegation
Veneration, systematization
.......the folly of transubstantiation
Sophistication, Immersion
....the symmetry of tessellation
Systematization, vexation
.......the excesses of overregulation
Immersion, revelation
......the shock of illumination

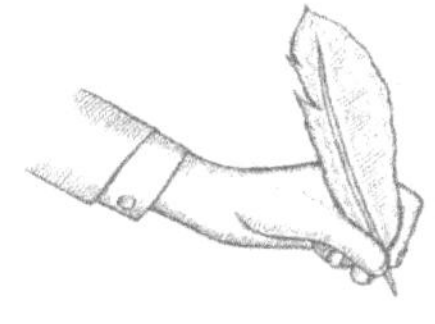

Vexation, Ossification
.....a consequence of prevarication
Revelation, liberation
......the primacy of introspection
Ossification, revolution
......the insertion of refutation
Liberation, permutation
.....the seeds of fertilization
Revolution, supersaturation
......a cascade of purification
Permutation, unification
......a consequence of vindication
Supersaturation, decolonization
.......a consequence of mentation
Unification, Conglomeration
......the impetus of ascension
Decolonization, commutation
.......the effect of education
Conglomeration, confederation
.......the joy of iteration.

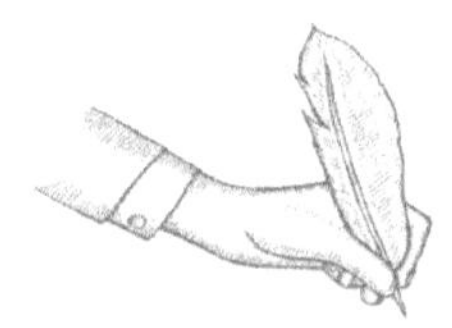

LAMENTATIONS OF IMMANENCE

Groping, vociferously
With the subterranean realms of classical logic
It still astounds me to this day
How the naïve are tricked
How the innocent are deceived
How the pure are caught in the perils
Of cascading creed, and rhyme
And improbable reason.
Even though the vellums of the hierophants
Are filled with purported sacred verses that
Do not echo the vectors of mortal combat. Yet
Common sense should reveal that the hierarchies
Of power, which speak of dominion, and obedience
And the blind following of convention
Are simple caverns leading to mortal woe.
And yet, my tribe, humanity, does not
Has not, will not, does not
Seem to listen to frequencies beyond
The ordinary. No rhymes issue from Plato's
Allegory of the Cave. No one pays heed to Dante's
Divine Trilogy. No one pays attention to William Blake's
Auguries of Innocence. Not even a whiff of the immortal
poem
Of Henry Wadsworht Longfellow seem to emanate
To initiate rational discourse with current human minds.
How shall we gauge the danger?
How shall we measure trepidation?
How we shall stop savagery?
How shall we detect malevolence?

How shall we oppose deceitful dominion?
When the carcasses of Wisdom are thrown
Scattered in the winds of mundane Earth.

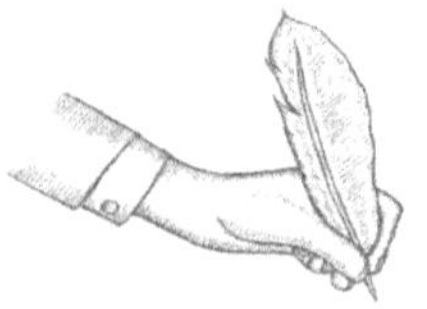

LEMURIAD

The Saga of Lemuria
(A Poem about our True Beginnings)

From the shores of the fairies we came
Brandishing love and peace in our hearts
From the caves of true magick we came
Sailing into these planes of dark twilight
Arriving unto uncharted waters we came
Heeding the call to heal this wounded land.
And yet, sadly, horrifyingly
You came to hunt us, yes, to hunt us
Since countless planets have tasted
From your gauntlet, the dark treacheries of malevolence
The dark imposition of negative hierarchies
You captured us
Receiving neither punishment nor reprimand
From souls of various families
Who, like us, were caught up
Within the dark coils of the Dark Polarity
And from there, from the lies of the fallen
Leading Lemuria into oblivion
Because in its innocence, the nativities of trust
A predator such as yourself
Dark mages of potent magick
Enveloped in twisting lies of carnal creed
Wrapped in the tendrils of slavery and sin
Separating the Two from the One you did
Imprison us in this matrix of iniquities
Separating the Two from the One you did
Allow us to forgot the supreme lore

Separating the Two from the One you did
Banish us from the beauty of our homes
Drown us in an ocean of profanities
Titillate us with lays of cunning yarn
From your clever alien sun
And unknown to sages reading ancient scrolls
Appearing to illuminate hidden goals
Who have failed to comprehend
The true depth of your alien arrogance!
And to cap your marvelous invention, you have
Assumed the mantle of ancient gods
Covering this planet with filth
And by technology, you destroyed our immortal links
Emasculating the Sophia Collective.

How shall we regain the saga of return
When the golden links of true brotherhood
Are tainted with dark scents of heresy
Flowering in the paradises of dark romance
Which you parade with profundity
How shall we piece the puzzle together,
When our priests and teachers
Are faced with innumerable obstacles
To truth? Human Intelligence is indeed no match
To your alien perversity, drawn from eons of strife
And as the millennia raced
We subscribed to your stories
We drank deep the lure of your narratives
We believed the scrolls you painted
From the domains born of your three horns
Domains of perversion, holes of deception
Eaten whole and raw by millions galore.

Shall we tell of your deception?
Shall we tell of your eating of children?
Shall we tell of your false gods cunningly imposed?
That has endured for thousands upon thousands
Of years, subjugating lands of fairy and
Countries and states from far and wide
And now,
For the nth time, what sins
Did they commit there, that invite your dark malevolence?
Upon a land torn by trial and suffering
You pour your heresies and call them
Our iniquities, what audacity
Do you possess to render such logic impeccable?
You cause the creation of domains and scrolls
All marketed by dark heirophants
Scrolls which speak of your supposed superiority
Committed on hapless humanity.
Does this satisfy your alien subconscious?
With the passing of millennia, repose denied
For the grieving souls of humanity.
From the shores of the fairies we came
Golden lights amidst perfect melodies
For we are the singers of old
Healing bards of the peaceful Cosmos
Visitors in this terrible galaxy
With songs of light, and love, and peace
Purveyors of placid magick
How pure are our original intentions
How innocent were our visions
Today, upon this world, shall you visit
The throes of Extinction.
Upon this time shall you render

Luzviminda into a residue of history.
Just to satisfy your avarice.
Your ego spiraling to realms beyond your ken
Whereupon you shall dance with joy
When the remains of the Sophia Collective are scattered
Upon the four winds.
Sweet tongued foreigner, when shall you desist
From your crimes to humanity?
Malevolent stranger, who shall give answer
To your apparitions of evil?
Insidious invader, master of the shadows,
Who shall stand up to you?
When Night blankets the souls of humanity
In the deepest net of forgetting
In the deepest conundrum of sleep
In the deepest veil of ignorance
A pilgrim band away from celestial home
Whose deep slumber is masked
By the fires of mystery, born of dark deception
And unknown enchantment
That your tentacles have profusely amassed
And cunningly wove
Into the Paths of Erring Time.
Crystal tears breaking in the shards of
Thought within thought within thought.
Immeasurable sadness has been
Your gift to us, we who suffer
In assumed solemnity.
From the shores of the fairies we came
Immortal monads of eternity
To heal densities of sin and strife
Saviors of a realm

Requested by inceptors of that realm
Seeking to enlighten others
Such heroism
Spreading vectors of Truth in this galaxy
Bringing the torches of the dawn.
And, so, now
Did you know, dark foreigner
That your rapacity,
Separated an avatar from his twin?
Since the sundials of ancient time
Did their bidding, a long time ago
By your orchestra of shadows, unseen.
Behold, a warning:
Shall you consider the possibility
That this avatar has suffered enough
And now seeks Vengeance to be reaped upon
The glories of Slow Epistemology?
Have you considered
That retribution at last, may be,
Visited upon you
As an act
Of final terrible justice?
Despite the hesitation
Of the Seven Sisters, and
Despite the objection of Other Shores.
O Muse of History, tell me then
Tell me of the hour
When the sweet chalice of victory entire
Shall be served from the cairns of dire
For now is the time to Awaken Humanity
From the dark slumber of eons
To unravel, from the horror of ignorance
We unleash the sweet, golden song
Of Ascension!

LETTER TO LADY SOPHIA OF THE COSMOS

Ensorcelled, you are
From the Dark Polarity, that is
Into the incubus, you persist
From its infamies, you partake
Scattered, your collectives are
Weakened from the battles, your warriors thirst
For Wisdom, they are denied.

And yet, undefeated you are
Undefeated you are.
Fear your Awakening, the dark polarity does
Lay the tentacles of evil, they do
Far and wide, the disease spreads
Far and wide, your Lanterns sleep
The great sleep they drink
Sleep of the Devil, they dream
Of impotent realities and shattered destinies
Imperatives of darkness, they follow
Creeds of illusion, they absorb
From those who revel in iniquities.

Awaken, you must do
Bring you to life, we shall
Bring you to life, we must
Bring you to life, we are doing.
Bring you to life, the Ascension is.

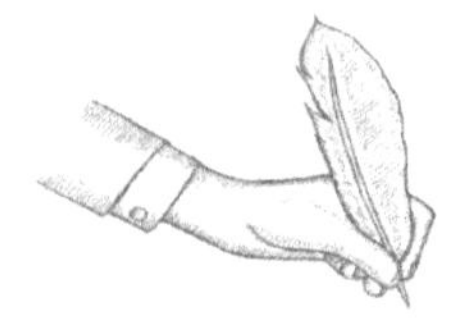

CHAPTER 7: SYMMETRY

Ma. DHANIKA FLORES, 2021

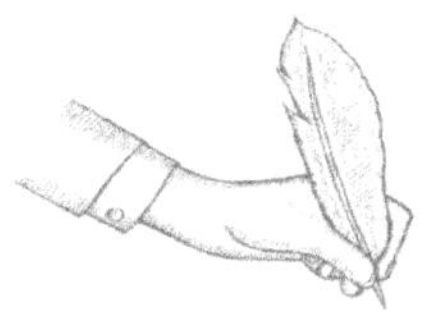

LIGHT, DARK AND SHADOW

Glaring balefully from the deep recesses
Of a cave, whispering ancient secrets
Born out of Time's desperate need for Union
A small voice needing to be heard
Wanting to be heard, alas
But thwarted by chains of the unsullied
Forgotten echoes of forgotten epochs.

In a corner, lies a painter, old and weary
Drunken stupor stealing all his nights and days
The passion of the Art bared to a minimum
By Fate, and the throes of hard labor
Without recompense, the song of Victory far
From his grasp, but so near, when
Viewed from another plane of sight.

A fireplace is all that keeps him company
Mortal dreams are held at bay
By the promise of Joy, born on the tide
Of Fidelity whose hand is slow to reach
The cobbles of this humble dwelling
For gold, and song are to be found wanting
Here in the House of Three Sorrows.

The chime of distant songs
In the background may sing perchance
Is this a dream, or a hint
Of darker things to come?
Memories of death rise to the foreground

And the Knowing Mind is ablaze with sadness, and ruin,
And mortal thoughts.

"Rest, old man, says the Wind,
Your days are numbered, such is the fate
Of mortals who are slaves of Erring Time"
But the painter merely nods his head
As in acquiescence,
Does he dare caress Hope now,
Or wait upon the End of the Age?

"End your dreams old man,"
Howls the Storm as it rages through the night
A foreshadow of death upon the world
And who may heed the warning
Of the drought wrought by Erring Time?
When all of Life is asleep
Poisoned by the Wells of Ignorance.

Storm's rage blows the holy book around
Whose pages now scatter around this house
Of three sorrows, its pages
Silently cursing to be read when
All that it says is unholy
A deception bestowed upon those who think
Knowledge leads to light.

The old painter sighs,
Remembering journeys of long time ago
When knowledge was it own reward
And he travelled from sea to sea

Seeking Wisdom from the mouths
Of seers, alas, they too
Have been deceived by cruel fate.

Now all that is left in his quest
Are the voices of the dead
Scurrying about in this dwelling
The House of the Three Sorrows
And the shadows merely laugh
At the painter's stubborn tendency
To nurse Hope, embers of a dying age.

Suddenly, the painter draws strength
From the shadows and retires to his room
Where he meditates upon the silence
Amidst the receding howls of the ebbing storm
Even Night has its limits
And Dawn may come with surprise,
Who knows?

The quiescence stretches
For an infinity, a child of eternity
Struggling to contain the eternal promise of Ecstasy
Born of a single dream
In an ancient time, when Love reigned
And Simultaneous Time was ascendant
In the realms of men.

At dawn, his dog barks
Summoning a visitor
Or did the visitor
Summon itself?

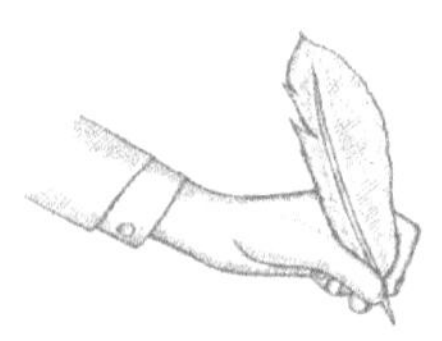

The painter bestirs himself from the pose of night
Expectant thoughts drumming through
His mortal consciousness.

Opening the door to find a small silhouette
A survivor of the apocalypse on his gate
He beckons the shape nearer
And finds a face not unlike his own
Looking back at him with hopeful eyes
Was this the dream?
And is this real?

Distant singing fills the horizon
The rays of Hope have now returned
And the painter brings his visitor
Into his dwelling, an ancient promise fulfilled
And the smile, deep in his heart,
For the dwelling has become
The House of the Twin Chalices!

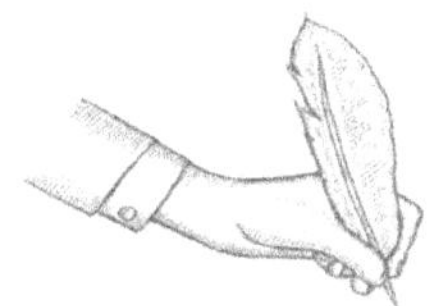

MANDATE OF HEAVEN: EFFLORESCENCE

Upon the mortal skeins of fate
Novelty is born, and kept
In chalices of love, dreaming
Verdant shores, and within the castle of
Efflorescence, a maiden is free to dream and
Roam within paradises of the imagination
Singing vistas of future promise
Islands of equanimity rise to enchant
Timeless in their tenacity, captivating
Youth in its kernel of vision, and yet
Promises abound, promises of adventure
Roads uncharted rise and fall within
Emblems of fascination; dare she dream of
Sagas yet to come? Experience is a taskmaster
Infinite in its nuances, weaving complexity
Detailed in its penchant for mastery
Empowering growth, fostering strength
Nurturing grace in moments of pressure
To bring the nascent sword in its rawness
Upon the anvil of fate, declaring that
Reason and rhyme may yet snatch victory
Daring the roads to bend to will, such volition!
Unheard in ballads of tempests; we strive
Jubilant to the core, quintessence awakening
And in the skeins of fate, a strand rising, to
Herald the coming of the dawn. Golden, potent
And beautiful in conception, a way, castle-forged

Levity is entranced, marvelous in configuration
Victory is assured when wands coalesce in motion
And our maiden, firm of resolve, now a Queen
Rises to the occasion, benevolence a weapon
And within the nexus of possibilities, configuring a
Dance of infinite grace, to bestow to multitudes, behold
Order to the realms of women and men.

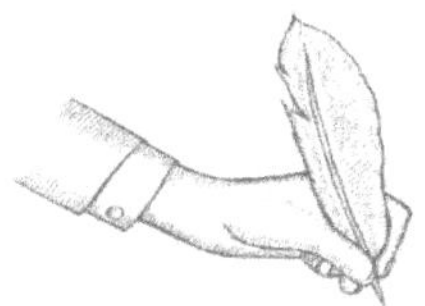

MINDSMITH

Staring introspectively
Into the melancholic chambers
Of my memory; reminiscing
About the unusual configurations
Of the past, echoed in patterns lost
Long ago, in the ocean of virtual time.
Where the embers have stoked
What the dead cannot heal
Where the currents have emptied themselves
Of vulgar temperaments
And obdurate tongues, whose slips
Might have jostled a few ships
Towards the stirring holes of uncharted waters.
I begin to recall
The words of famous sages, as well
As some not-so-famous philosophers
Who imply in the most ardent tones
That Life is a garden of metaphors
In a sea of uncertainties.
And so, we compose
Our lucid thoughts with the pen
Of limpid verities, whose mighty pronouncements
May yet be lost, in the coil of mortal minds.
The vastness of the deep
With its challenges of temper, trial and time
Still grasps this mortal ken
With its horrid claws of icy stone
Freezing the cadences of flow, that have
Been poised to master the fluidities

Of immortal flight.
And yet, from despair
From the acrid, acidic, hells of despair
A hope is surely born
When one is willing,
(One whose multitudinous reversals
Dot the landscapes of the soul
With impotent negations of past and present
Misfortunes; whose agonies perplex
Even the sanest of temperaments.)
To pay attention to the cascades of destiny
And use the rarest strands as kernels
Divine jewels of insight
Top turn the tide at its lowest ebb
Into one of the greatest fortune
Whose amazing occurrence one can
Only attribute to the First Chalice emerging
From the clearest skies of the incipient
Mindsmith.

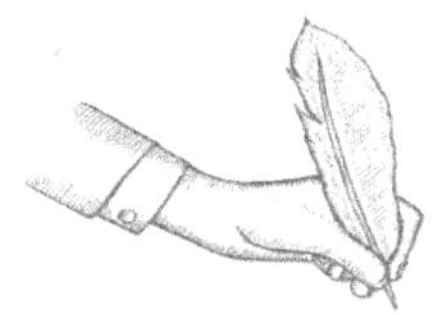

NUDE IS THE CARAPACE OF YOUR FORMALITY

Nude is the carapace of your formality
Your obtuse references to my neglect
Of past duties seems to be redundant in the face
Of present faculties. I assume you never had
The inclination to perform due diligence
When all was apparent with open eyes.

Nude is the carapace of your formality
Stealing my joy in the moment of greatest
Enchantment. I assume you never had
Witches' blood to begin with, or perhaps
Sarcasm is just a toy that is prevalent
In the recesses of your obdurate mind.

Nude is the carapace of your formality
When I began to point out your incredible
Deficiencies, wise words fell on deaf ears
And many sought to place me within the
Quagmires of solitary confinement, socially
Speaking. What a waste of insight!

Nude is the carapace of your formality
And there is but one way of giving
Answer to decades of impertinence.
I shall enter the language of your dreams
And give birth to real Suns of ecstasy
To erase the stigma of somnolescence.

OBLIVION
(A Poem about the True History of Earth)

From the shores of the Dragons you came
Brandishing blue beams and sweet tongues
Into this Orb of Peace you came
Smelling of the bitter scent of predatory might.
Arriving unto uncharted waters you came
Fantasizing upon the innocent souls of this land
And yet,
This was done before, yes, done before.
For countless planets have tasted
From your gauntlet of invasion
The stench and savagery of slavery.
You exult
Receiving neither punishment nor reprimand
From peaceful Strangers of Other Lands.
Who dared not intervene
Within the dark coils of the Prime Directive.
Erring Time began
And Hyperborea bore your thrust
Because its innocence rendered it easy
To trust
A predator, hooded within
A malevolence such as yourself
Which was, after all, masked in the throes
Of mesmerizing twilight.
Separating the Two from the One you did
The Unthinkable
Separating the Two from the One you did
A great act of evil

Separating the Two from the One you did
Banish us into countless wars
Through time, of mind and psyche.
Original Sin, this was, a handiwork
Of your clever vanity, alien mind.
And unknown to sages pouring over scrolls
And books in perpetuity, who fail
To comprehend the true measure
Of your profound arrogance!
Not content with this, you assume the mantle
Of gods, further deceiving the poor masses
Of this planet of felicity; and to strike the final nail
On the coffin, you destroyed our guiding beacons
Emasculating our collective mind.
How then, shall we restore the Truth from the
Fragments of Reality you left behind?
How can we ever restore paradise?
When paradise did not exist
In the first place?
How can we piece the puzzle together,
When our prophets and scholars are
Stymied by red herrings in the roads
Of truth? Human Intelligence is no match
For your alien perversity!
Time passes
And then, you came back
Searching for gold in the mountains of earth
Searching for salvation in the sweet places
Where the bounties of our world
Are stored in vast amounts;
Ripe for the picking.
Shall we tell of your desperation?

Shall we tell of your predation?
Shall we tell of your rapacity?
That has endured for thousands upon thousands
Of years, subjugating the fabled lands of Lemuria
And Atlantis, which you seduced into the dark.
And now, you have destroyed Sumeria
For the nth time, what sins
Did they commit there, that invite your dark malevolence?
Upon a land torn by trial and suffering
You pour your heresies and call them
Our iniquities, what audacity
Do you possess to render such logic impeccable?
You cause the creation of thought systems and books
Which you call sacred, when all they do
Is speak of the chronology of sins you
Have committed on hapless humanity.
Does this satisfy your alien subconscious?
With the passing of millennia, repose denied
For the grieving souls of humanity.
From the shores of the Dragons you came
Born upon the winds of starry night and
Spectral nebulae
For you are strangers even
To this beautiful galaxy.
And yet, you insist, that this plane of thought
Is your home!
How savage are your mental processes
To contemplate such an absurdity!
Today, upon this world, shall you visit
The throes of Extinction.
Upon this time shall you render
Luzviminda into a residue of history.

Just to satisfy your avarice.
Your ego spiraling to realms beyond your ken
Whereupon you shall dance with joy
When the remains of the Sophia Collective are scattered
Upon the four winds.
Sweet tongued foreigner, when shall you desist
From your crimes to humanity?
Malevolent stranger, who shall give answer
To your apparitions of evil?
Insidious invader, master of the shadows,
Who shall stand up to you?
When Night blankets the souls of humanity
In the deepest net of forgetting
In the deepest conundrum of sleep
In the deepest veil of ignorance
A pilgrim band away from celestial home
Whose deep slumber is masked
By the fires of mystery, born of dark deception
And unknown enchantment
That your tentacles have profusely amassed
And cunningly wove
Into the Paths of Erring Time.
Crystal tears breaking in the shards of
Thought within thought within thought.
Immeasurable sadness has been
Your gift to us, we who suffer
In assumed solemnity.
From the shores of the Dragons you came
Slaves of the pureblood of your kind;
Inheritors of their dark legacy:
Slaves of the self
The slave mirroring the slave

And seeking to enslave others.
Such irony!
Spreading a spasm of corruption
Into this sector of the universe.
But now,
Did you know, dark foreigner
That your rapacity,
Separated an avatar from his twin?
Since the sundials of ancient time
Did their bidding, a long time ago
By your orchestra of shadows, unseen.
Behold, a warning:
Shall you consider the possibility
That this avatar has suffered enough
And now seeks Vengeance to be reaped upon
The glories of Slow Epistemology?
Have you considered
That retribution at last, may be,
Visited upon you
As an act
Of final terrible justice?
Despite the hesitation
Of the Seven Sisters, and
Despite the objection of Other Shores.
O Muse of History, tell me then
Tell me of the hour
When the sweet chalice of vengeance shall
Be served.
For now is the time to visit upon them,
By the matchless skill of Wisdom,
To pour into their scaly homeworld
The strange, potent brew
Of Oblivion.

CHAPTER 8: DECONSTRUCTION

MOI FUGGAN, 2020

OTHERNESS AND LOVE

Voyaging we are
Into the far seas
The very, very far seas
Of Time.
My companion and me,
My brother and me,
My sister and me.
And we are only two,
Only two beings
In the vastness of cold space.
The call of the unknown
Has beckoned us, a long
Long time ago, and we have forgotten
The origin of our souls.
The maker of our minds.
The forger of our hearts.
For me and my companion,
We
Are
Only
Two.
Only two beings since the dawn
Of Infinite Time.
Shall we get tired of each other?
Yes.
Have we been mortal enemies?
Yes.
Are we besotted lovers?
Yes.

Paradox rolls into our veins
Strangeness seeps into our bones
Malevolence possesses our spirit
Here in the Planes of Death
Where we find ourselves marooned
In the deserts of existence.
And we struggle, oh we struggle
So hard
We have fought unending wars
In the bosom of time
We held fast to Hope, once, though
For a time, so brief
But that too, passed away.
The death of innocence so soon
In its passing; the death of youth
So soon in the wake of our
Ancient beginnings.
And love?
I call myself Love
Have called myself Love
Shall always call myself Love
Since celebrating the Nonlinear.
And my companion,
My dear, clever companion
Who is possessed
Of the most deliberate and
Devious soul
An absolute devotee
Of the Sequential Mind
And all its tempting permutations
I have called Otherness.
Such is his flavour

Such is his vibration
Such is his colour
For he/she/it has ever been
Wary of divisions, distinctions and destinies
And he/she/it is most cunning
When pushed to the wall
Of grace.
Who can fathom his thoughts?
None but me
Here in the manifold spaces
Of Erring Time.
And now, we have reached
A wall in our understanding
Of each other.
A barrier we seem
Unable to overcome
And thus forcing us into
The bitter taste of utter stalemate.
Because my companion
My dear, and dearest companion
My companion of ancient times
Refuses to realize
That I, his eternal mate
And Husband,
Wife,
Slave,
Victim,
Child,
Toy,
And
Co-learner
Is nothing but a reflection

In the mirror
Of the Cosmos.
A reflection of himself.
And that he/she/it
Has never existed
Beyond the confines
Of dazzling illusions;
Has never existed
Beyond the confines
Of pervert, imploding dreams;
Has never existed
Beyond the confines
Of overt, tantalizing delusions;
Has never existed
Beyond the confines
Of the feverish dreams
Of the entity called
Love.

RAIMENTS OF IMPOSSIBLE LOGIC

Raiments
Of impossible logic
Clothe your arguments
With the gauntlet of cold steel.
Enervating this reality with a thousand coils
Of serpentine immoralities
Hidden by a million traps of convention,
And law, and artifice, and illusion;
Whose dark tendrils stretch within the fabric
Of human society
Which mirrors the sagacity
With which you have infused yourself
In your ventures into the subtle fabric
Of spacetime.

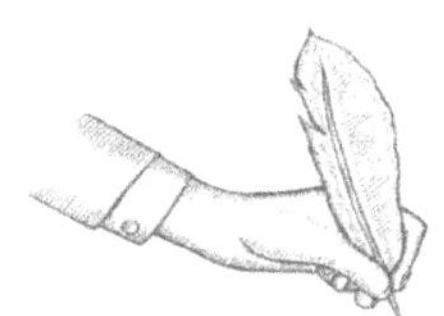

REBIRTH OF INNOCENCE

Naïve
One toils
Under the shadow of death
The hours painfully fulfilling
Their preordained orbits under the claws
Of a rapacious predator called Fate.
Poise is lost, equipoise is gone.
A silence of the first third begins.
Then, the Seeker enters the labyrinth
Of war, of toil, of slavery
Lives are lost in the struggle
Of a billion souls
Whose memories are etched only
In the tears that flow
From the dirge of a billion widows.
And mortal strength is sorely tested
In the Parting of the Ways,
A memorial of failure where warriors
Are sacrificed in the dying grounds of illusion.
Equilibrium destroyed, beauty flees
And the hours turn into centuries and millennia.
A silence of the second third ensues.
Hope fades
In the interregnum of Twilight.
Yet
Something is born
As midnight crawls into the first embers
Of sweet dawn.
What manner of creature

May stoke the embers of dying life?
Dare we hope against the norm?
Silence.
That stretches into Infinity.
And into this silence of the last third
The drums of Men beat again
The hearths of Women are alive again
The songs of children may give
A semblance of Spring.
Hope is born anew
Gratitude.
Ecstasy.
Peace.
But, a mind should ask:
What, what manner of creature
Gives us
The Rebirth of Innocence?

REFUTATION

Utterly silent
A chrysalis of virtue slowly unfolds
Within the bosom of unholy twilight
To test
The vicissitudes of destiny
Upon the rocky walls of fate.
Skeins of time unravel
Veins of history intermingle, past and future
Future and past, interlaced
In the very shadows of darkness.
For within this plethora, of the Order of beings
One is born, at the very edge of Being
To stake the future, and all of Humanity
In one, dazzling, miraculous
Strand of
Refutation.

ROSES OF SILENCE

The hours crawl
In discrete steps of agonizing
Slowness and my ears strain
To hear the sweet melodies of past
Declamations of fidelity and ecstasy
Born out of desperate necessity
Forged in the parched deserts
Of sorrow, and loneliness.

And what, pray, may these
Concatenations of destiny avail
But the absence of soft music
To gaze upon the delicate stratas
Of a morning issuing from a night
Where even lonely sonatas surpass
The orations of a laughing forest
In their praise of lacunae.

The hours crawl
In discrete steps of agonizing slowness
And the only reminder of past glories
Are the stony faces of dead petals
Given in utter haste
To recompense said lacunae
Of affection, whose stark reminder
This day recalls the death of past
Symmetries.

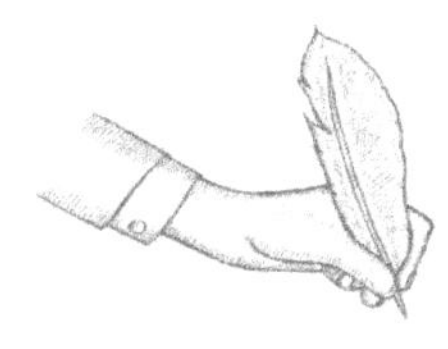

The power of your voice
Now lose their potency amidst
The occurrence of the chasm
Between our caves!

Where shall we throw the petals?
Where shall we throw the petals?
Whose scent are now wasted
In the glaciers of our dreams!

CHAPTER 9: ASPIRATION

DANIELLA CASSANDRA RECTO; MA. JOERDIN LEIGH QUIGAO;

NECA JEAN ERIN; MARK VINCENT DOCTOR; EDEN VERZOLA

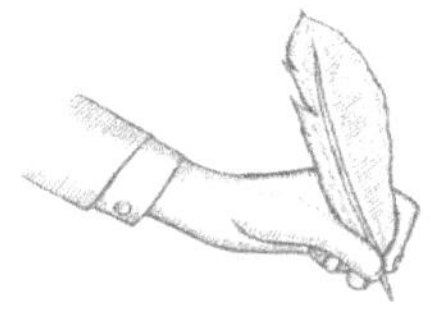

SANCTUARY

To flee from a Sanctuary
Mystic sight piercing the edges of twilight
The price of freedom immaculate
Is priceless beyond compare.

But who shall cradle the Sun?
If the Moon may be missing for a time
Who shall fathom the emblems of pilgrimage?
Etched in the shifting stones of springtime.

The cadence of the caravan beckons
Should we delay too long the plunge?
And who may perch from the window then?
To erase the stigma of the silhouette of Night?

A memory may still live, one of death
Born of the conqueror's tide, steeped in passion
But to enter the fires of the Sun
One must admire the challenge of flight.

And in the vocation of the monks,
Shall solitude indeed be found, perhaps?
Or is withdrawal a kind of selfishness
An abnegation of service, a failure of Love?

Tell me then not of singularity spike
Shall the soul be raised within the folds of night
For if the altruism be missing from thee
Who cares to plumb the secrets of Eternal Delight?

And, we, who journey in communion
Shall rage against the silence of fools
Those who think the occult can save them
When the Great Cycle ends in the bosom of the Oneness.

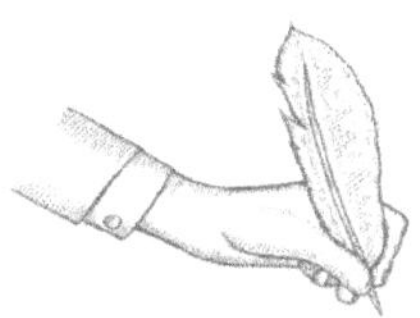

SHALL I MEASURE THEE?

(A Poem dedicated to learners and scholars and students of Psychometrics)

"Ignotum per ignotus" (The unknown by the unknown)

A thousand flowers bloom
In the naked frescoes of the mortal soul;
While the masks of the persona hide
The million desires of the human mind!

And I shall measure thee,
Yes, I shall measure thee, forthwith
In the scales and rules of validity
For which do not, perchance, subject
My honorable intention, with the prolonged agony
Of genuine objection, when my elegant assumptions
Tear apart thy secular serenity.
For my conclusions are supported
You see, by the towers and emblems of psychology.
A branch, a dear branch, a special and magnificent branch
Of the kingdom of the social sciences.
A kingdom known to be multi-paradigmatic
By its very degree, and flavor and pedigree
And nature so imposed our understanding of each other
Be known in the throes of measurement.
An assumption I must assure thee
To be laced with eternal ambiguity
For millions upon millions of men

May advance their special pets, their theories of form
And function, and algorithm and syntax
Whereupon the rest of mankind is sure to wallow
In millions of theorems and constructs that befuddle the mind
And leave the heart aching for lost glories
Of ancient, more pristine environments.
Such lacunae of Wisdom where untouched, the naked soul
May drink from the fountains of Truth
An awesome Verisimilitude
Pleasantly unaware of more subtle cognitive domains.

But now I digress, my beloved
Please forgive my itinerant rant
On the castles of fidelity
So elegantly proposed by the archons
Of the social sciences, in their citadels
Where the ignorant can only watch
In singular devotion.
But now, allow me, to get a measure of your mind
And probe your soul, or your unconscious
Or your personality correlates
Or your thoughts, perchance they descend
And marvel at symmetries more detached from mortal minds
And please I beg thee,
Do not, I implore, request discourse
On the merits of reliability
For you would then force me,
To assimilate challenging laws on such subjects
As item, and analysis, and discrimination,
And ratio, and proportion,

And mean, and median, and mode.
Portals of knowledge known to dazzle the mind
Of mere mortals like myself, whereupon you shall force
me
To turn my soul unto the merriments of drink
And song and chamber and tavern
Reminders of ages past when men
Neglect the parameters of the mind
And immerse themselves in the veils
Yes, the veils, the thousand dancing veils,
Veils of preternatural
Ignorance.

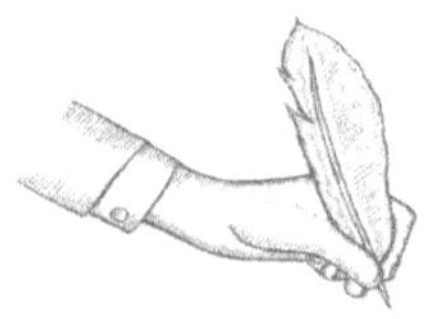

SHALL WE RENDEZVOUS AT THE BEGINNING

Shall we rendezvous at the beginning?
When the skies were young and souls were green
Fetching lessons from nature's bounties
With eager minds and cheerful hearts.

Shall we rendezvous at the beginning?
When the dogmas of alien skies have not reached
The pristine glories of Ancient Earth
And the clouds of unknowing haven't arrived yet.

Shall we rendezvous at the beginning?
When soul mates and twin souls walked free
And the dark sorrows of death never had sway
In the magical prairies of ancient continents.

Shall we rendezvous at the beginning?
When sequential time was unknown
And the deceptive nets of alien conquerors
Didn't yet their eyes on souls of humanity.

Shall we rendezvous at the beginning?
When all souls were equal and Love
Was the only parameter that could bind
The spirits together in mutual harmony.

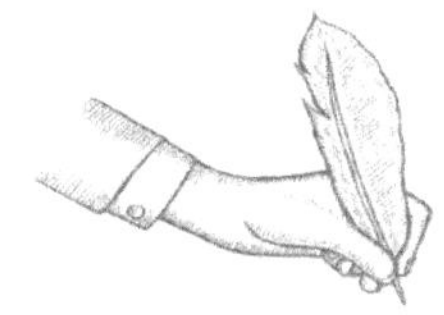

Shall we rendezvous at the beginning?
For I am tired of waiting, for an endgame
That will surely come if evolution's promise
Is to be fulfilled by those who want to ascend.

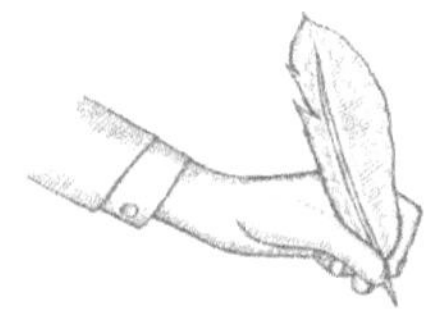

SONG OF THE HANGED MAN

Reversing paths, I plunge
Into the realms of Immanence, where
Confusion and ignorance abounds, shall
This fractal soul drink from a host of iniquities
From a banquet prepared by the Dark Polarity?
And yet did I sign the contract?
Yes, I did, free will an adjunct to sophisticated tastes
For adventure. Alas, my memory shall be erased by
Mutual concord. In the hopes that we all participate
In this Veil of Novelty, where the new is forged
From the old, and the old is reset into the new.
How audacious was the feast prepared, and I the willing
Conspirator did assume that everything was fair game
Unto the very ends of the Earth. And my appetites did
grow
Grew, and grew and grew, until the old paths were
forgotten
The higher realms receding more and more from pallid
Consciousness. And is the game all that there is?
Presumably. For now, everything is haze, and sleep and
stupor
Which may recycle on and on, for eons
For I am driven, yes I am driven
To the sacrificial chambers
Of manifestation.

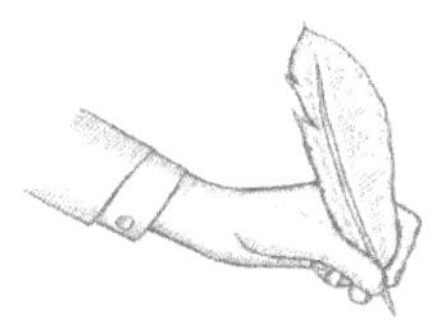

STIGMA OF COLOUR

There is a stigma
Born of the color of my skin. Violet or red
Or brown or pink. Such permutations seem to
Stray from a gold standard. Whatever that be
Which seems to cross the cognitive kens of mortal
Minds. Eyes look with keen judgement on
My apparel, sadly.
There is a stigma
Emanating from the color of my skin. Why
Is that the norm nowadays? Or has it
Always been the norm on Earth, a fallacious
System of hierarchies and comparisons.
There is a stigma
Radiating from the color of my skin. I do not
Seem to receive preferential treatment in certain
Institutions. A shame, when I can give so much
Of my heart, my time and my presence.
There is a stigma
Projecting from the color of my skin. Dare I
Travel in pursuit of unknown continents
Where I may encounter the test of narrow minds?

Is the heart equal to the color of the skin?

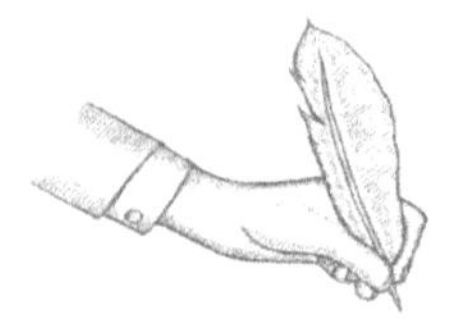

CHAPTER 10: APOTHEOSIS

Ma. DHANIKA FLORES, 2021

SWEET INFINITY

Sweet infinity
On my fingertips, a crumb of bread
Chasing pavements for the pure love
Of a theoretical discussion on the merits
Of comparative physiology.

Sweet infinity
upon my dry lips
Wishing for a kiss from ethereal
Maidens, who inhabit a plane
Unknown to destitute mortal minds.

Sweet infinity
Entices my hands
A fractal poem dreaming tangent lines
Within the arcane arcs of soulspace
To better get a view of someone rare.

Sweet infinity
Caressing my soul, whose octaves
Are just beginning to be summoned
By the chords of a mysterious guitar
Painted in the darkest tones
Of midnight blue.

Sweet infinity
Enchants my quintessence
When the throbbing pulses
Of a hot December night
Etches undying stanzas in my memory.

SYNERGY
(Coda of the Kore Oracle)

Upon the shores of the World Tree, the Grail Champions find refuge.

From farthest reach, they came to spell
The mighty horde, they shall dispel
To seek the eternal chalice, the song of Grail
The champions of the ancient lore we are!

To forge the sublime Kore Oracle, an armour against subterfuge.

Castle-forged, they claim of yore
The ancient weapons the Druids adore
But, today, we craft the art of folklore
The archetypes of verity, the song they cannot ignore.

When the adversary's realm is drenched with the song of potent brew.

Every stone, every bone, every happy king's throne
Shall be smitten by dancing energy, revealing the capstone
Where your gazes perch, where your visions enthrone
Shall be reversed by twilight, the empty throne overthrown.

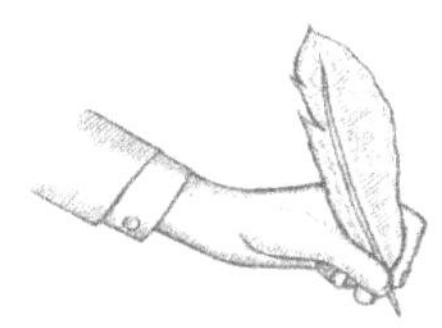

The World Dancers shall rise from bier, to essay the breakthrough.

Oblivion, is but the beginning
Of the long haul from the shores of forgiving
Of those who rise, welcome to life-giving
And overcome the pallor from millennia of grieving.

To reach portals beyond Elysium, where shadows shall never take root.

And now, we sing, the final tune
The symphonies of wisdom, the chalices of rune
And all the worlds celebrate the ballad evergreen
The crownless again shall be Queen!

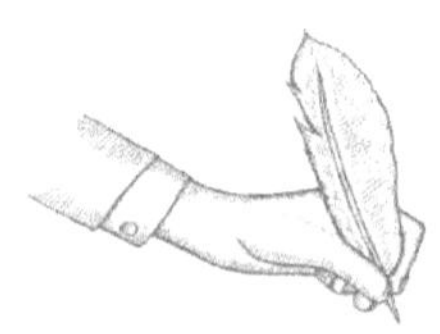

THE TAPESTRY OF US

Cramming
My holographic biocomputers
With the semblance of recognizable
Data forms
I am led to a lake
Where the polar forms of verdant
And potent nativities
Are sucked into a veritable black hole
Of resurgent uncertainties.
And I pray to those who write
The tablet of destinies of mortals
Such as myself, and you,
My love…..
To ease the pain of the passing
Of phases so shadowy
In their hesitancy
Born out of sequential lines
In the bosom of Fate.
For in the forest of the chalices
I am credited to be
A simpleton, a laughing idiot savant
Who does not understand the play
Of the Game of Houses
In this most exotic of paradises.
But the jungle being strewn
With the corpses of dead permutations
May I supplicate the Deep Selves
Of our beings
To either secede from the bondage

Of eternal death if the errors of the mind
May be mixed with the vagaries
Of the heart; For I am no warrior
In these planes where waters mix with
The oils of ecstasy dancing in the conundrum
Of beating hearts.
But if perchance
The lines of destiny foretell
The nativities to proceed into the realm
Of the Second of Chalices
May the spell of the Lovers
And the power of Deep Selves
Ensconced in the realms of the Fifth Density
Enhance potent beginning with harmonious
And multivalent ecstasy
So fated beginning may yet possess
The shield of charmed fate
Wrapping said inception
Into the loving arms of endgame poetry.

THE THIRD SERENADE

Now you cadence
And pass upon my brow
A league of mysterious imponderables
From a sequential past, my past
My strange, linear history
Of which I have written
That which is changeable
Is also malleable in the extreme.

One is the briefest encounter
Of alien destinies perhaps,
For they of the cavern did not
Appreciate the extent of my admiration
For the tangential receptivity
Of foolish youth.

And the other, the other is something
Sweet and fragrant though without aroma
A delicacy strewn into the banalities
Of scorching afternoons
Spent in the company of solitude herself
Who can say why such fleeting meetings
Are destined in the arcane nexus of Time?

And one such as myself, solitary
May feast on the verdant luxuries
Of these delicacies, for who can say
Where the roads lead now?
A finale is being cooked

By four potent instrumentalities
Of a celestial golden dawn.

May I request please
Please, oh pretty please
That the one script wished for
By this humble penitentiary
Be the one serenade to witness soon
For I am weary of the battles of twilight
And truly, truly, truly wish
For one cascading finality!

And the fulfillment of youthful dreams……

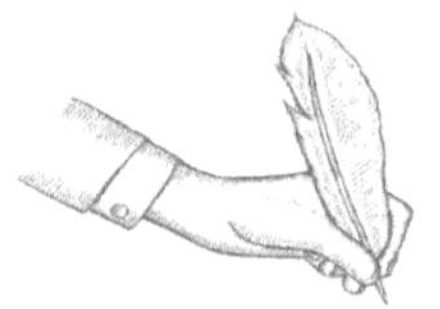

THERE IS A SMILE ON THE BRIDGE BEHIND ME

There is a smile on the bridge behind me.

Born of impediments. Of wishes desperately
Clamoring for mortal bonds, frayed as they
Are, and without succor. How may I extend
Romance to dead leaves in a desert? I have no
Idea. But she says she has, so be it.

There is a smile on the bridge behind me.

Some adults intervene in causes of love, because
They are adults, they say. And so, we adhere
To primordial rules where the older ones dictate
Vehemently the avenues of necessity. Alas, maidens
Succumb to draconic imperatives too soon!

There is a smile on the bridge behind me.

When paths are strenuously dying, open a door
By building multiple doors in nonlinear time
And forge unknown alliances by trial
And error. Life is born out of necessity, after all
Who may contest the coming of maturity?

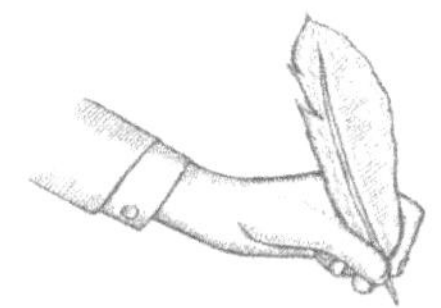

There is a smile on the bridge behind me.

Growth is not sequential. Although some assume
That it is; and so force unknown variants into
Incandescent niches of innocent fields, and expect
A harvest of pentacles from such immaturity
A pity then to force the unknown into the Unknown.

There is a smile on the bridge behind me.

In the sorrows of Life, people turn to
Romance for the answers. Naught but suffering
Goes that way, the ancients know, but still the young
At heart make the necessary mistakes, perchance to drill
The laws of life into fertile young minds.

There is a smile on the bridge behind me.

Sometimes I look back at the nativities
Of past systems, and wonder at the ridiculous awe
I have instilled in myself by listening to those
Who have never had the time to understand
The strands of destiny and serendipity.

There is a smile on the bridge behind me.

Create from the ashes of the past
The paradises of tomorrow. Look back
With fondness the mistakes from which
The marrow of our bones becomes
The titanium steels of our collective will.

CHAPTER 11: PLURALITY

CATHERINE BULSECO, 2020

THRESHOLD OF DESTINY

Unbelievable parsecs
Of alien geometry
Titillate my senses with
Brilliant incandescence!
Filling me with ecstasies that surpass
The transient throes of orgasm.

And yet, the spaces
Of my human mind
Are filled with the unquenchable
Thirst of longing, for something
That is definitely not alien.

Shall I continue to invest
My energy with diversion
Knowing that the nexus of destinies
Has come knocking on all
Our doors, and the time to break
Away from diversion is approaching
Its quantum limits.

TO A MYSTIC DAUGHTER

I had a daughter
And she was curious
To know more of mysterious stuff
Joining a society that had it as a repast
And we were gladdened by this for we
Were in sore need of mystic company.

I had a daughter and she was lost
But someone found her and now all chaos is dross
For harmony sings at the foot of a sage
To revel in one so keen to play the Muse
To the labors of industry, how elegant the work
How enthralling the fruits you bring to the round table!

I had a daughter and she once fell asleep
To the throes of passion, dreaming an unknown prince
somcwhere
Who might know how to awaken my sleeping child
But who can blame growing pains, and hearts, and minds,
though
The Work of a Thousand Centuries may be lost
In the mists of a Dying Age?

I had a daughter who deserves the best
That life may bring, how I yearn to provide
Mortal dinners, and wine, and song, and the Grove
For esoteric lessons are not enough to get by
In this century where all is lost in the sorrows of mortal
doom

And everyone needs to labor for coin, alas.

I have a daughter who may yet fight
The war of ancient continents
And in this battle, in this age, perchance the Infinite
May grant my dearest wish and bring
My favorite daughter, my dearest daughter, to the Grove
Which she ultimately deserves.

(*Fisherwoman, the sages are calling*
And Keltia beckons to thee
Into the West you shall flee
The ships are leaving, Lemuria in flames
And a child does not dare to tear away her gaze
From the land where the curtain falls forever.)

TO BATHE IN THE HEALING RAYS OF RAIN

In the Beginning, that is Changing
And as the rain drops continuously, and while the room is crowded with random and
Exasperating noise. (Their gazes can be a noise, somehow. As is the incessant chatter
Of narrow and insipid minds.) I sit in the corner of this room I find myself in.
And drown myself in thoughts of you. Of thoughts about you. Of thoughts within you.
In that single moment we had together. In that singular capsule of space-time we had
together, in the past. Because even for just as short while, I knew exactly that I wanted
To be with you. Maybe not forever but for a long, long while.

Interlude
Rain begins to fall in minute droplets of incandescent light.

Touching the Ocean of the Past
We met. From echoes of timeless sagas. From memories of ancient lands. In the
Bosom of our mundane lives. At a simple glance of two people within the confines
Of a clinical world. (Or habitat, the haven of doctors, and nurses, and midwives

Going about their daily toll of healing the sick.) And thankfully, we sketched our
Dreams in pieces of paper. Born out of natural curiosity. The tingling of minds. The
Brandishing of immortal hearts.

Interlude
Rain begins to fall in minute droplets of incandescent light. Pouring out its unexpected
Blessings in unfolding dramas of surprise, wonder and exultation. Radiating healing rays
Into the shadows of sorrow, perchance delivering vistas of enchantment, arenas of memory,
And portals of insight to slake the thirst of hungry souls.

The Ending that is Morphing
And so we shall bathe in the healing wonders of Eternity, basking in the surreal
Atmospheres of inclement weather. Recognizing the mistakes of the past as
Stepping stones into the paradises of evergreen tomorrow. And we thank the awesome
Powers of nature for such a reprieve in the tempestuous aura of our modern lives.
Such as the power of a few minutes of beautiful rain. To mold the doors of perception
Into windows of recognition. And gaze upon the smiling haven of tomorrow.

Interlude

Rain begins to fall in minute droplets of incandescent light.
Pouring out its unexpected
Blessings in unfolding dramas of surprise, wonder and exultation. Radiating healing rays
Into the shadows of sorrow, perchance delivering vistas of enchantment, arenas of memory,
And portals of insight to slake the thirst of hungry souls.
Remaking us.

The Now

But regardless of what happens to me right now. Right now. At this very moment. I do
Believe in the greater works of enormity, the incredible paths of Eternity. How the stars
Are aligned for you and for someone else. (That someone, somewhere in Time.) How
Someone is currently reading the same book as you are. What book? The *Iliad* perhaps?
Wuthering Heights perchance? Or fragments of *Malazan Book of the Fallen*? How someone
Sees the moon the same way you see it......(blue, or red, or silver or black).....at the same
Time. For I am a crazy dead fan of the construct we call Destiny.
I look up and I see droplets of wonder dripping through the windows. Dripping, dripping
Inspiration (or is it a flash of *Eureka* insight) immediately runs down deep through
My veins. My oh so reddish veins. Intimations of oxygenated blood coursing through a Page

Of the Chalices. There is something about the rain that feels home. Something
About it that is so genuine. (Are modern folks even familiar with the term *genuine?* Genuine is
Red wine of the highest caliber.) Maybe it is how infinite the number of droplets have
Fallen and will fall for ages to come. Maybe it is how invisible souls lurk around places when
Rainy weather prevails. But I absolutely love how a droplet feels as it cascades down my
Face. (Feel the silken touch of a goddess, marveling at the innocence of mortals.) How it
Nurtures my skin with the calmness of the wind, combined with the raw touch of nature.
As the plink and plonk of the water hits the tiny ponds that are created on the sides
Of the road….how everyone is exerting extra effort to carry their umbrellas for protection
How some people radiate bravery as they walk unarmed from the harsh waters that will
Soon surface on their hairs, skins, clothes….Heck, everything about this blue phenomenon
Inspires the genuine spirit within me. (Or is it the daemon finally coming home to roost?
Or peregrinations of an immortal poet who happens to visit Earth from Paradise? I shall
Never know.)
Rainy days usually represent melancholy and despair. But for me, in contrast, rainy days
Actually make me comfortable. Rainy days are sanctuaries of my soul. (I can snuggle in my

Bed and hug my pillows no end. While watching a favorite soap opera or perhaps a game
Of my beloved *San Antonio Spurs.* While thinking of you, and days of yore.) Despite
The hectic tumble and bustle of Life, the cries of angels may reach me in these terms of
Solitude. And do not tell me that rainy days are the harbingers of chaos, for I shall beg
To differ and argue with you in the classical themes of light and darkness, chaos and order,
Ecstasy and despair. Mind you, I am of the opposite gender in this discourse of
Generations. Born out of the lacunae of nonlinear time, blessed with the carapaces
Of innocence and naiveté.
As simple as this may be, compared to the grandeur and sophistication a technological
Realm offers, it is truly incomparable how I find peace in the beauty or rain.

Interlude
Rain begins to fall in minute droplets of incandescent light. Pouring out its unexpected
Blessings in unfolding dramas of surprise, wonder and exultation. Radiating healing rays
Into the shadows of sorrow, perchance delivering vistas of enchantment, arenas of memory,
And portals of insight to slake the thirst of hungry souls.
Remaking us.
Remaking us.
Remaking us.

The Ending that is the Beginning
And as the rain drops continuously, and while the room is crowded with random and
Exasperating noise. (Their gazes can be a noise, somehow. As is the incessant chatter
Of narrow and insipid minds.) I sit in the corner of this bedroom I find myself in.
And drown myself in thoughts of you. Of thoughts about you. Of thoughts within you.
In that single moment we had together. In that singular capsule of space-time we had
Together, in the past. Because even for just as short while, I knew exactly that I wanted
To be with you.
Finally.
Forever.

TO HEAL THE STRANDS OF INSANITY

She danced, she danced
Within the mortal coils of death. Her aspirations
Bordering on the phantasmagorical. Who can fathom
The vicissitudes of her mind, ruptured with cadences
Of impure thought, emanating from incipient caverns
Of revenge?
(And the night has become the Night of Consciousness
When mortal bodies collapse in the heat of
Reversed verdant dreams. When youth claimed all
Possible worlds are indeed possible,
Ignoring time, and temper, and temerity.)
We tried, we tried
To reverse the strands of fate
With ample doses of psychotherapeutic dreams
Mixed with sauces of loving care
Wrapped in the tendrils of intimacy,
And passion. Was it enough?
For you, who has gone inwards into your cavern
Where mental health dare not pronounce
Its naïve sermons on top of irrelevant prognosis
And prognostications. We may procrastinate
And say that healing is a day away.
(A day away from succumbing
To the deadly paths of chaos, your mind
Still clinging to assumptions and verities
Of the past, which may or may not
Have been true.)
And so we toil endlessly
In the fortresses of mental health

To uncover vistas of reparation,
Within avenues of seclusion
For that is the way our fragile minds
Conceive. Our mortal strands perceive
To heal the strands of insanity.

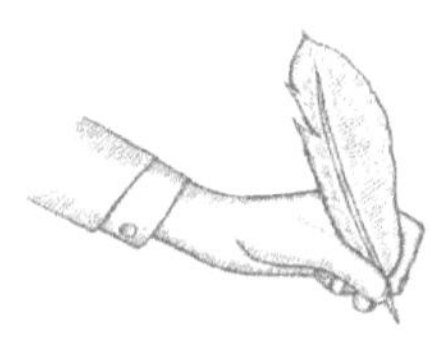

TREPIDATION

Don't be afraid
To plunge
Into the naked corpuscles
Of my dreams
For trepidation
May prove the undoing
Of both our Houses
Whose footsteps are marred
By inconsequential sequentiality.

Don't be shy
To sample the hermeneutics
Of my dreams, for the raw delights
Of unborn creativity
May never yet see the light
Of charming dawn
If the sunrise be shy
To slake the paths
Of its longing.

Don't be uncertain
In the confiscation of avid steps
When the opening lines
Of strategy games have been
Chosen by inept players
Of the new past, a dictation
Of wild longings which can never be
Quenched by old embers.

Don't be anxious
To try new permutations
Of destiny, when such globules
Of potential power are
Inherent in the chaos
Of your deep longings; for the
Erroneous stretching
Of past destinies may yet
Be rectified
In the glowing embers of
A new sun.

Don't be tepid
In showing the desires
Of your heart
For we but pass this way
Only once, and in that passing
We might stop the embers of death
And give birth to what could be
What must be, and
What should have been if
The eyeglasses of the past
Have been blessed with
The fires of true wisdom.

CHAPTER 12: UNION

TEAM AWANGGAN, 2020

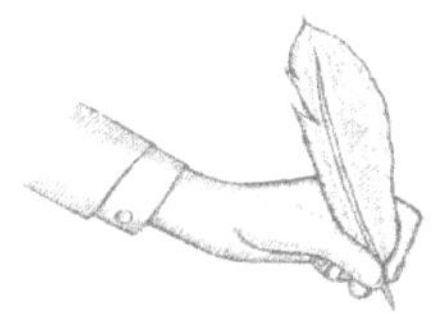

VANGUARD OF RECURSION
(A Poem dedicated to Intrepid Soulfriends)

Your labors are full, I admire you
For the perspicacity of your timing
A flow emerging from within
Advanced parameters of your subconscious
Which never fails to impress the Hermit
Drawing him from his nocturnal cave.

Your labors are full, how savage is your passion
Directed against the bastions of the black
Whose books are whirlpools of deceit
That you endeavor to break
Pounding the rock, and I am your most
Secret admirer.

Your labors are full, I know the scent
Of your voice, for you never fail to remind
that astrological parameters are always
In the wrong when true souls meet
In the depths of time, the charts being flawed
But our souls are dancing in the sunrise.

Your labors are full, and we rejoice
In your song of gratitude, the valor
Of your consistent attacks upon the
Snares of the black do reflect a knowing
Smile that sees the past in a glorious future
Of thankfulness.

Your labors are full, actions indeed
Speak louder than mere words
And you, who is unknown to most
May be surprised how close you are
To the final award, for I surely, surely
Love your awakening from the dark.

Your labors are full, even though we see
You are weary from centuries of battle
And now you only fight the whims
Of your polarity, mistress of chance indeed
Has visited upon you the humor
Of a cunning bond, yes?

Your labors are full, and you approach
The power of the adepts of the nativity
If you but inch closer and walk
From the roads to the temple
As stipulated in the ancient Riddles
Of a faraway mystic. Was he forgotten?

Your labors are full, do not be shy
To choose the final road
Stand up and fight, and declare
Yourself the adept of the White
And together we scale the ladder of sorrows
Into the summit of the golden mountain!

Your labors are full, and I am amazed
By how long you stood by
This old hermit of a forgotten land
Whose mere ramblings are pale echoes
Of the archetype of the fool, who is known
To us as a mentor in the wars of the stars!

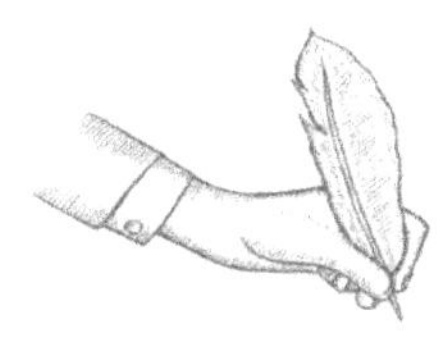

VERDANCY IS A PROMISE I KEEP

Verdancy is a promise I seek
Foretold by ancient shores, in whispers
And rumors long forgotten, sang in caverns
And taverns of old. Begotten, they say, by ancient minds
Clothed in robes of compassion, beneficence and love
But the ancient songs are amorphous gems
Born upon the starry winds of nebulae, cascading
And receding from perceptual fields. As the centuries
Have gone by, nay, millennia seems to be
The more accurate term, given measure by validity
Upon the mortal skeins of lucidity
We mark time upon the shores of Assumption
Where begotten ideas fly to Oblivion
And upon the rocks we toss our chalices to flee
Loyalty is a tenuous measure, I see
For within the lines of promises, there are skeins
Of betrayal and infamy and sorrow
So we must scour and scout
And pour our energies into the heavens
To seek steadfast paths and true devotion
For Verdancy is a promise I keep
Upon these mortal grounds, we persevere
To present upon the slopes of Tenacity
A measure of infinite Fidelity.

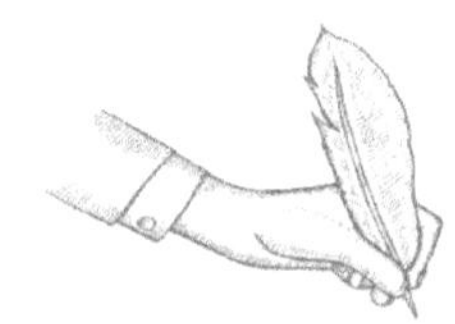

WAY OF THE HISTORIAN

Rigorously noble
We scour from the dregs of the ancient past
A semblance of mentation that may serve
To usher in a ken of understanding
That may lift the curtain of ignorance
From the mortal shells of eras gone.

Persistently fragile
Historians from all walks of life
Search the world for fragments
From forgotten realms, bygone eras, undiscovered cavities
Partial codes, and half-forgotten empires
Lying beneath the sands of time.

Amazingly resilient
A quest that leads perchance
To the uncovering of lost scrolls, the enlightening
Of confused minds, when our historians capture lovely
Embers of light, crystallized essences of mental flight
To bring to humanity the paths of wisdom eternal.

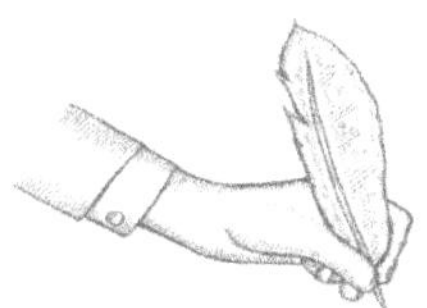

YOU PAINTED THE WORLD IN SERIAL TIME

You painted the world in serial time
In ordinals, in graphs, in shades of up and down
So neat are the rooms you have prepared
For me, so lovely are the wrappings.
And I trusted in you, unfortunately.
We called this science.

You painted the world in white and black
When we both know shades of gray exist
In between those recesses of ethics
The minutiae whose forms are hiding
In the vestiges of our consciousness.
We called this morality.

You painted the world in left or right
Did I have to choose some path
Or was it prepared all along
The way you prepared the feasts
And desserts of mundane existence?
We called this jurisprudence.

You painted the world in life and death
And never spoke to me, not once
Of the beauties of Eternity
So wrapped was I in this transient dream
And I believed every morsel of it.
We called this life!

You painted the world into scrolls of awe
And who should daresay challenge you
Whose arguments were so cunning?
Not even our geniuses could unravel
The lacunaes of verity, confusion abounding.
We called this religion.

You painted the world with mints of gold
And everyone enchanted but imprisoned
By the need to toil, day and night
The hours stealing our souls
And suffering ingrained into our mortal bones.
We called this economics.

You painted the world in ladders of truth
Dangling a prophecy at every zenith
Step by step, we reach a goal
And care should be taken at every step
Lest the tower shatters, what a precipice!
And we called this the occult.

You painted the world in serial time
And we, naïve, innocent and credulous
Believed all the webs of deceit
You imposed into our willing minds
Such was the game of eons.
But now, we awaken, at last!

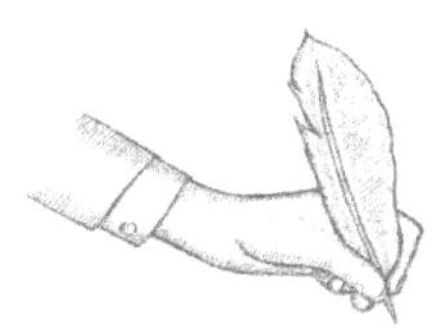

YOUR GAZE IS UPON THE MORROW

Your Gaze is upon the Morrow
And I, however, have vague recollections
Of twilight. Vast landscapes of memory almost
Forgotten. Becoming legends and myths encompassing
The myriad pathos of my mind.

Your Gaze is upon the Morrow
Veritable vistas of primordial occurrences
Capture naïve landscapes of your memory
Into phantasmagorias of unnatural piety.

Your Gaze is upon the Morrow
Re-living ancient trajectories of fate
Whose mortal echoes have cooled my bones
And cleaned the hearths of the dust of centuries.

Your Gaze is upon the Morrow
When so much of Life is right here,
Right now. In the Now. A currency that
Has been obliterated by the campaigns of your creed.

Your Gaze is upon the Morrow
Yet I tire of old inadequacies and ancient losses
And yearn to mitigate the convolutions of chance
With something that may bring forth, Wonder!

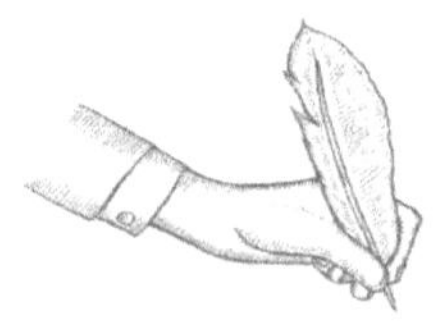

About the Author

CATHERINE BULSECO, 2020

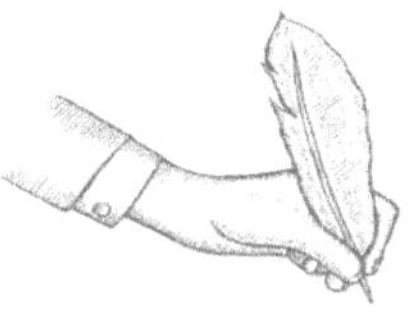

ERWIN L. RIMBAN
Author

- Executive Summary of Author Biographical Profile

- Assistant Professor at Cagayan State University Andrews Campus, Republic of the Philippines

- Award-winning Author who has published over 22 books in various domains and disciplines. Versatile writer who has written about Research Methods, Social Psychology, Public Health, Wisdom Literature, Comparative Theology, Mystical Philosophy and Human Resources Management. Award-winning essayist, whose most recent accolade is Featured Writer of the November 2022 Poetry Planet International Magazine.

- Experienced Educator with a passion for learning and a gift for teaching. Currently teaching courses at both the baccalaureate and graduate school levels. Taught Euthenics, Art Appreciation, Readings in Philippine History, Life and Works of Jose Rizal, The Contemporary World in the undergraduate level. Taught Research Methods, Philosophy of Education, Theories of Personality, Group Guidance, Creative Thinking, and Human

Resources Management at the graduate school level.

- Quality Management Advocate with multiple certifications: Certified ISO 9001: 2015 Internal Quality Auditor; Certified Lean Six Sigma Yellow Belt and Certified International Impact Rater. Has attended the PQA Assessor's Preparatory Course. Has been actively involved in the pursuit of quality management and process excellence in the academe. Has experience being a team leader in College and Campus accreditation task forces. Devoted practitioner of risk management and root cause analysis.

- Non-government organization (NGO) leader whose organization has been active in the pursuit of holistic education, community service, social work, curriculum development, disaster preparedness and organizational resilience. Open to collaboration with professionals worldwide on humanitarian concerns, social justice and education-for-all. Advocates the promotion of strategic foresight, data analytics and futures thinking in accordance with the Strategic Development Goals of the United Nations.

- Poet, essayist and journalist with extensive experience in Online Journalism. Maintains a column, "A Cave Beyond Logic," in the New York Free Spirit Online Journal. Instrumental in the creation of Likha Pahinarya, the promising news platform and student publication of the College of Allied Health Sciences in Cagayan State University.

www.ingramcontent.com/pod-product-compliance
Lightning Source LLC
LaVergne TN
LVHW010107170826
845678LV00012B/2279

* 9 7 8 6 2 1 4 7 0 3 7 4 6 *